Endorse

I know what you're thinking…*Stars! that is astrology! And that is bad!* And yet, the Bible says God made the heavens and the earth. Genesis 1 says it was He who put the stars in the sky. Do you think there might be something to God's heavenly order? Stars are mentioned over 50 times in the Bible. True, the enemy has tried to steal the stage when it comes to the heavenly hosts with horoscopes just like he has with the rainbow. But Troy Brewer has put forth a book that is going to blow you away. He has done his homework and the revelation comes flying off the pages. Let's set things straight when it comes to the skies above, and may you shine among those who need Yeshua *"like stars in the sky"* (Philippians 2:15).

RON CANTOR
CEO Tikkun Global
President Shelanu TV, Tel Aviv

This is my kind of read! *Looking Up* by Troy Brewer is such a key book to expand our thought processes. The Word of God goes out on lines around the earth (Psalm 19), and Troy is one of the few people I know who can explain how the delivery of the Word of God works from beginning to the end. This book will cause you to see you are a part of the universe–not just a person on earth. God is Lord Sabaoth; the Lord of the Stars. He is over the Host of Heaven as well as the Army in the earth. Few people understand how the stars work on our behalf, but this must-read book will break open new ways of seeing! Get beyond any religious thinking you have and allow *Looking Up* to help you comprehend that you are part of the bigger picture. God demonstrates His great faith by putting man on earth to war in and with the heavens.

DR. CHUCK D. PIERCE
President of Glory of Zion International, Kingdom Harvest Alliance, and Global Spheres Inc.

In his book, *Looking Up: How the Heavens Declare the Glory of God*, Troy Brewer shows how God has consistently used astronomy to reveal Himself. Troy offers a unique perspective on some of the most notable events in human history, including the birth of Christ and His triumphant return at the end of time. Troy culminates his study with a look at Jesus' return and God's final victory, as declared by the signs in the heavens.

JIMMY EVANS
Founder and President
XO Marriage

Troy's book reminds me of the quote from the great reformer and president, Abraham Lincoln, who said, "I can see how it might be possible for a man to look down upon the earth and be an atheist, but I cannot conceive how a man could look up into the heavens and say there is no God." Truly the language of the stars is shouting the glory of God. Troy Brewer is a master communicator and storyteller who shatters the silence of mere stargazing by unlocking the language of Heaven written in the stars. He makes the glory written in the stars accessible to the common man.

DAN MCCOLLAM
American author, speaker, and co-founder of
Prophetic Company, Bethel School of the Prophets, and
the Spiritual Intelligence Institute

Troy Brewer is a powerful, end-time voice desperate to share the unadulterated Gospel of Christ with boldness. *Looking Up: How the Heavens Declare the Glory of God* is a prophetic blueprint, bringing radical change to a hurting and dying world. Anyone and everyone who is praying for a mighty move of God needs to grab hold of the truths found in this book. Open your heart, mind and your spirit to receive what the Lord is saying through these pages. As you apply the revelation found in this book, you will be completely transformed by the glory of God and the power of the Holy Ghost.

BRIAN BOLT
Senior Pastor CityReach Church

For centuries, satan has orchestrated a massive cover-up concerning God's prophetic message in the stars. In this book, Pastor Troy Brewer rips the cover off and reveals the mysteries that God has placed in the heavens. You will be challenged and you will be changed as you dig into what will be one of the most unique books you've ever read. Every end-time warrior needs this book in their arsenal!

ALAN DIDIO
Host of *Encounter Today*

Looking Up: How the Heavens Declare the Glory of God by Troy Brewer is something that culture needs right now. This generation has been given a substitute through astrology and the new age that is printed, Tik-Toked, and even used for corporate personality types. This counterfeit is hidden in plain sight almost everywhere. Troy helps us understand the true voice of God that often comes with signs in the heavens. God has powerful and even perpetual prophetic messages for us that we can attach our faith to every day and it helps to ground us not only in what to look forward to today, but to understand Jesus and

His Kingdom. Wow! Troy brings so many signs, types of ways God speaks, and almost clinical but practical and fun understanding to the nature of God through this book! You will be armed with the right equipment to have conversations with friends, family, and even other Christians for how to go after the supernatural but also to reject the counterfeit!

SHAWN BOLZ

Bolz Ministries

TV Host, Podcaster, Prophetic Voice, Author

LOOKING UP

BOOK ONE

PROPHETIC SIGNS IN THE CONSTELLATIONS AND
HOW THE HEAVENS DECLARE THE GLORY OF GOD

TROY A BREWER

Destiny Image® Publishers, Inc.

P.o. Box 310

Shippensburg, PA 17257-0310

"Promoting Inspired Lives."

This book and all other Destiny Image and Destiny Image Fiction books are available at Christian bookstores and distributors worldwide.

For more information on international distributors, call 717-532-3040.

Reach us on the Internet: www.destinyimage.com.

ISBN 13 TP: 978-0-7684-7195-3

ISBN 13 eBook: 978-0-7684-7196-0

For Worldwide Distribution, Printed in the U.S.A.

1 2 3 4 5 6 7 8 / 27 26 25 24 23

Contents

Constellations

Zodiac Constellations

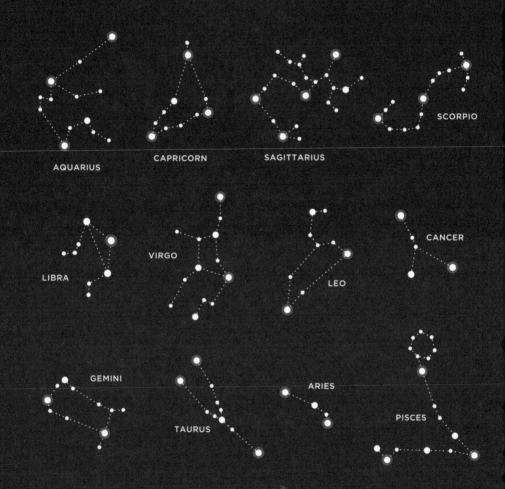

AQUARIUS

CAPRICORN

SAGITTARIUS

SCORPIO

LIBRA

VIRGO

LEO

CANCER

GEMINI

TAURUS

ARIES

PISCES

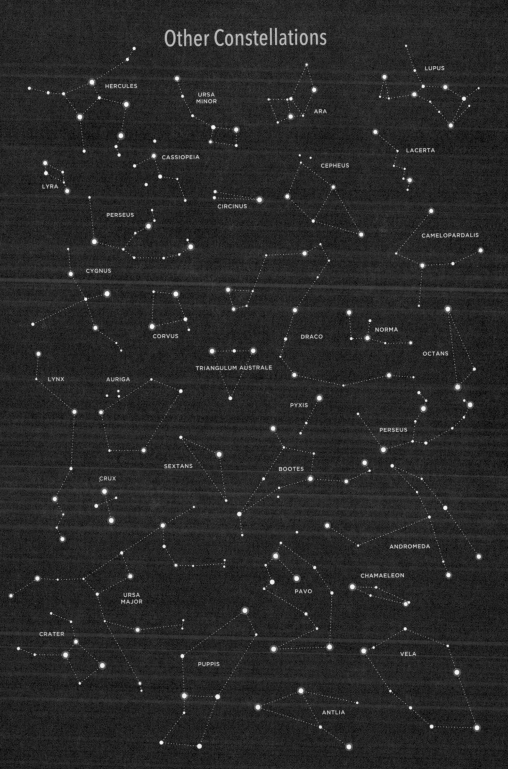

For Leanna

My Cassiopeia, seated upright. My queen and heavenly bride.

Nearly 40 years ago we went on our first date. I didn't have any money, so I took you to a cow pasture, pointed to the stars and then did my best to woo you with my guitar and serenade you under the heavens. I must have sounded like a hillbilly tomcat. You pretended you were interested in my astronomy. I pretended I knew what I was talking about.

It was the first time we prayed together. I remember it as some kind of starry amphitheater, and it seemed like every star in Heaven was applauding our prayer. I drove out of that field certain I had found my wife and certain we would both be in trouble if I didn't have you home by midnight.

We are not teenagers anymore. The story of redemption has cycled and rotated more than 30 times since that first night together and we are still together and still looking up.

You have been telling me for over 20 years I need to write a book on this subject. Since it took me so long to get with the program, I am going to write several.

—TROY BREWER

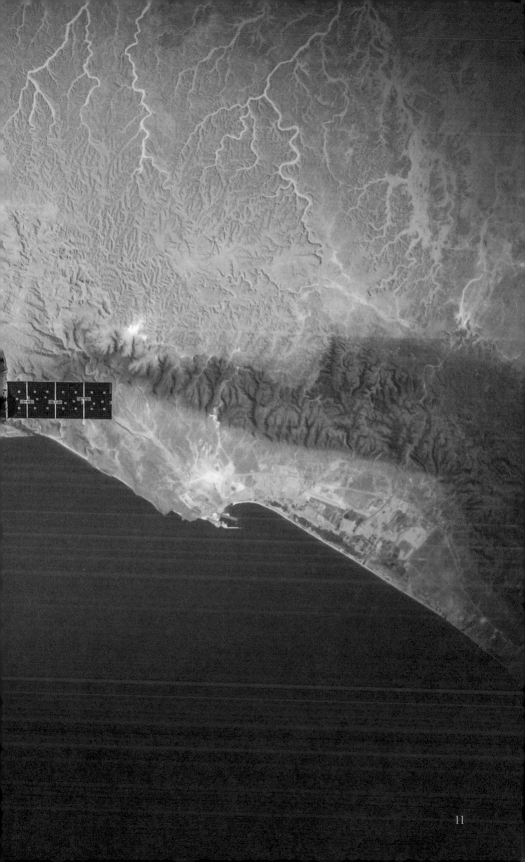

Foreword

My dad would come get me on weekends and sometimes he would take me to the Fort Worth Museum of Science and History. As a little boy in the mid-1970s, Fort Worth was a long way from rural Johnson County, Texas, in terms of geography and in culture. While we had the cattle sale, football games in Joshua and a Dairy Queen, Fort Worth had the zoo, TCU, The Colonial Golf Tournament, General Dynamics, The Southside Drive-In, a real subway into the Tandy Center, an ice rink, and the Cullen Davis murder trials. It was a very big deal to go to Fort Worth.

The museum was cool because it had things like dinosaurs and all kinds of Texas history, but the thing that blew my mind was something they call the Noble Planetarium. It was inside that little round room that I first learned there was a story being told in the midnight sky. I didn't know who was telling the story. I didn't even know what the story was, but I began to fall in love with the characters like my favorite TV heroes.

Orion was awesome, and there was even an Aquaman! The Big Dipper was undeniable and Sagittarius had his arrow pointed at the heart of the Scorpion. There was drama and there was the inside scoop reserved only for those people who were in the know. It was all perfect for a kid like me and I loved it.

1985 hit the world and so did my high school graduation. I was going to be a professional musician, live on the road, travel the world and spend the rest of my life with beautiful girls and friends on every continent. But in May of 1986, I had an encounter with the Lord Jesus Christ that changed everything. By the end of that same year, I was playing and singing in a Christian rock band, teaching the Word and feeding the hungry and homeless. I committed the rest of my life to one beautiful girl and we started doing ministry together. I couldn't get enough of the Word into my life. I couldn't have an experience with Jesus that was just too extreme. I wanted to dive into the deep end of all things prophetic, biblical and of the Kingdom, and that took me back to looking at the stars again. This time, instead of seeing the creation, I saw the Creator and His progressive, rotating plan of redemption, right there in the night sky. It blew my mind! It still does.

For the past several years, I have been hosting prophetic "Star Parties" as a way to raise money for our many orphanages, feeding programs, rescue homes, and mission projects that I and that same beautiful girl have throughout the world. I have also been teaching conferences on the same subject for at least two decades. It is a revelation so profound I cannot keep it to myself. I have to share it with a world searching for a savior. That Savior and His epic love story have been right over our heads the whole time. It's time the whole world looked up and saw King Jesus!

Light-Years and Star Wars

My intent in writing this book is to relay the stars and the way they line up as one of the many voices of God. I love God's plan and the extraordinary ways He is willing to declare His plan. I just flat-out love the heart of Jesus, so I can't help but love it when He speaks from His heart. Like I said before, this is an epic love story and y' 're a great big part of it!

I have to give a great deal of credit to the late E.W. Bullinger, one of my great theological heroes, for making this subject legitimate over a century ago. In 1893, he didn't have the web, search engines, or the great research work of many others to aid him. It's amazing what he was able to produce. His work is really what all the rest of us spring from when we reach for revelation on this subject. *The Witness of the Stars* from Kregal Publications is a must-read for those who love this subject matter, and one that I always refer to when I need brushing up.

I also want to thank and praise God for Pastor Howard Richardson from Gates of Glory Church in Dallas, Texas. It was under his teaching and anointing I first began to value the power of prophetic things. It was in a revival tent in Grand Prairie, Texas, back in the hellish hot summer of 1986 that I first felt Heaven's breath of fresh air hit me through this kind of revelation. Pastor Howard and this revelation changed my life. While the world does not celebrate him, I know Heaven does. I will be forever grateful for his profound influence on my life and ministry, and for introducing this subject matter to me as a teenage boy.

The Big Picture

As Bullinger says, there is no dispute from those in ancient times as to what the signs of the Zodiac are or even the constellations. As of yet, the American Astrological Society hasn't changed a constellation to the character of a transgendered person locked out of a mega-store bathroom. Though the world has changed, we still know what the pictures represent.

At the time of Bullinger's ground-breaking work, there was absolutely no question of the accuracy of the ancient star names, but we live in a different day. Sadly, men's efforts to leave God out of everything have brought many politically correct and watered-down versions of the meanings of the names of those stars. There will be none of that in this book, and if they don't like it, they can have Aquila dump a ton of water on them. Bullinger said in his day there was no dispute because these ancient star names were still preserved in every good celestial atlas. That's what I'm going for and will reference in the names of the stars, which are the details or the handiwork that David spoke about in the Psalms. I will also provide some of the biblical numbers associated with the light-years in distance and the size of the stars themselves. Bullinger didn't have that great luxury because those things were yet to be discovered, but the numbers are prophetic as well as the names. They help tell the breadth and depth of the story.

It is also my great hope that someone will read this and see the story for themselves. The story leads us to the beginning when the stars were created; and to the end when Jesus Christ returns to claim His title and redeem the entire universe. The creation leads us to the Creator. I hope somebody will hear His voice in the stars and give their universe to Jesus.

On a more personal level, I write this book in a busy time of traveling throughout the world rescuing girls and boys from sex trafficking, giving orphans homes, and pastoring an amazing church back home. The Lord has been so good to me in inspiring me and keeping me on course with finishing this project in the midst of so many others.

So thanks, Dad, for taking me to the planetarium. Thanks, kids, for letting me point things out to you in the midnight sky, and thanks again to Bullinger, Pastor Howard Richardson, and my tribe at OpenDoor Church in Burleson, Texas. Thanks to John and the revelation he wrote down 2,000 years ago. Thank you for your interest and for taking the time to pass this revelation on to others.

TROY ALLEN BREWER

The heavens declare the glory of God;
And the firmament shows His handiwork.
Day unto day utters speech,
And night unto night reveals knowledge.
There is no speech nor language
Where their voice is not heard.
Their line has gone out through all the earth,
And their words to the end of the world.

PSALM 19:1-4

CHAPTER
ONE

This Is How It All Works

The impossible logistics of simply
communicating a complex story
from Heaven to Earth

Let me introduce you to the challenge of communicating the greatest message in the universe.

So here's the rub. Somehow we have to have complex astrophysical engineering conversations using nothing but a still frame camera from 1996.... luckily the camera does spin.

Mark Watney from the movie, *The Martian*

I don't know that God has ever been afraid of anything. He's so profoundly confident. Unlike any other. So I would imagine it makes sense to say God has never been scared of a challenge.

He only had a dirty dozen, the 12 disciples, to take the message of the Gospel to the entire world. He has only had messed-up people in a messed-up world to partner with Him and line up with Him. He just doesn't seem to care what little He has to work with. He's amazing, and I love Him for it.

Another amazing thing about God is His extreme confidence in the hearts of humans. Though there has never been a day He hasn't been slapped in the face by all humanity, He still has this profound confidence in people. The Bible says in the famous Love Chapter that love believes all things and hopes all things. That is, love is selfless and always chooses to believe the best and hope the best. There is no protecting yourself when you are laying down your life and that is the kind of love the Father operates in. So He took on the unimaginable challenge of communicating His message to every tribe, every race, every language, in every location throughout every time frame. And He did it. He did it first by writing it in picture, name, and number form throughout the heavens.

Knowing the Plan

It is not that God wants everyone to know the plan. Well, He does, but not everyone is friendly, so He only wants those who qualify to know the plan. However, God loves everyone, so He wants everyone to be eligible to qualify. That is why the plan is in plain view for everyone to see, no matter where or when you live on this earth.

Jesus operates the same way. That is why He teaches in parables. Parables are stories that point to a real-life truth that is simple to understand. Just picture Jesus pointing to a farmer planting seed saying, "The Kingdom of Heaven is just like that." Everybody can hear what He is saying but only a few qualify for understanding—those who love and want to know Him.

> *This is why I speak to them in parables: "Though seeing, they do not see; though hearing, they do not hear or understand."*

> MATTHEW 13:13 NIV

Jesus spoke right in front of His enemies and said the same word that changed the lives of His followers. His enemies didn't get it.

There is a blessing in getting it and only those who qualify get in on it. As the Word says in Revelation:

> *Blessed is he who reads and those who hear the words of this prophecy, and keep those things which are written in it; for the time is near.*

> REVELATION 1:3

In nearly 40 years in ministry, I have traveled to nearly 60 nations. No matter where you go on this planet, there is a heavenly testimony proclaiming the goodness of God through the midnight sky. There are billions of Bibles all throughout the Earth where God's amazing heart and plan for redemption is given. However, where there are no preachers and no Bibles, there is the night sky. Before it was written in the Bible, it was written in the heavens. The author is the same. God's magnificent and mysterious plan of redemption is in plain view for everyone for all time if they are willing to *Look Up.*

Lift up your eyes on high, and
see who has created these things,
who brings out their host by number;
He calls them all by name, by the greatness of His might
and the strength of His power; not one is missing.

ISAIAH 40:26

How the Delivery of the Word of God Works

Let's talk about the logistics and mechanics of how God has chosen to deliver His Word to human beings. The Word of God is really who God is. It's His heart, and to receive His heart, you need to receive His Word. He gives us His Word in three different forms: the Written Word, the Spoken Word, and the Living Word. All three of these forms could be referred to as "books." When it comes to the written Word, God has written His book in three distinct platforms, all which testify of Him. First, He wrote His Word in creation (Romans 1:20), then in the pages of the Bible itself (2 Timothy 3:16-17). Finally, He has written His Word within and upon the tablet of our hearts (2 Corinthians 3:3).

"The Creation" book:

For the wrath of God is revealed from heav[en against all]
ungodliness and unrighteousness of men, w[ho suppress the]
truth in unrighteousness, because what may [be known of God]
is manifest in them, for God has shown it [to them. For since]
the creation of the world His invisible att[ributes are clearly]
seen, being understood by the things that are made, even [his]
eternal power and Godhead, so that they are without excuse.

ROMANS 1:18-20

"The Bible" book:

All Scripture is given by inspiration of God,
and is profitable for doctrine, for reproof, for
correction, for instruction in righteousness.

2 TIMOTHY 3:16

"The hearts of people" book:

Clearly you are an epistle of Christ, ministered by us, written
not with ink but by the Spirit of the living God, not on
tablets of stone but on tablets of flesh, that is, of the heart.

2 CORINTHIANS 3:3

One day, we will all stand before God and the books of our hearts will be opened (Daniel 7:10; Revelation 20:12). All that is written within us will be revealed and read out loud to the Glory of God. So the thing that you need to know is this: Before the Word was written in our hearts, it was written in the Bible; and before the Word was written in the Bible, it was written in creation.

This is the jaw-dropper for many Christians who don't read their Bible or refuse to search out the things in it they don't tand: A big part of the written Word in creation is what Bible calls the Mazzaroth (Job 38:32) or Mazzaloth (2 Kings 3:5). It's what the Greeks call the Zodiac, and that my friend, is what this book is all about—the Mazzaroth. We will debunk the teaching of the Zodiac and even take it back for King Jesus, so stay with me!

The heavens declare the glory of God;
And the firmament shows His handiwork.
Day unto day utters speech,
And night unto night reveals knowledge.
There is no speech nor language
Where their voice is not heard.

PSALM 19:1-3

God is speaking and one of the endless number of His voices is the signs in the heavens. It's never been a taboo subject in the Kingdom but the body of Christ has been driven away from this prophetic word by denominations, church boards and Christians who want to save other Christians from the heart of Jesus Himself. You are just going to have to get past all of the witch hunters and really go after God if you are going to enjoy this revelation.

The Zodiac: The Greatest Deception of Our Time

The devil has led more people to hell through the twisting of God's story in the stars than almost any other false teaching. What we know today as the Zodiac is his big rip-off of God's great revelation of Himself and His dwelling place in the heavenly realm. The horoscope? It's the devil's sick version of the prophetic voice of God as told in the New Testament:

But he who prophesies speaks edification
and exhortation and comfort to men.

1 CORINTHIANS 14:3

We were made with a homing beacon to remind us this rock is not our home. We were made to look to the heavens for the answer to who we are and why we are here.

He has put eternity in their hearts....

ECCLESIASTES 3:11

When we look up, we're supposed to be looking for Jesus in the supernatural. Instead, we settle for what we can see in the natural. The Word warns against worshipping the stars and looking to them as an oracle to plan and live out our lives by. The stars are very poor "gods." The Bible is very clear: to worship created heavenly bodies is wicked and God considers it idolatry (2 Kings 23:5; Deuteronomy 4:19).

If there is found among you, within any of your gates
which the Lord your God gives you, a man or a woman
who has been wicked in the sight of the Lord your God,
in transgressing His covenant, who has gone and served
other gods and worshiped them, either the sun or moon or
any of the host of heaven, which I have not commanded.

DEUTERONOMY 17:2-3

Mockers and scoffers, the ancient mystics, magi, false prophets—and after them, the Greeks—had no prophetic revelation of the story, especially where the story began and where it ended. They may have recognized there was a story in the heavens, but could they understand that story without knowing the author? Daniel makes is clear the answer then and now is, "No!"

> *Daniel answered in the presence of the king, and said,*
> *"The secret which the king has demanded, the wise*
> *men, the astrologers, the magicians, and the soothsayers*
> *cannot declare to the king. But there is a God in heaven*
> *who reveals secrets, and He has made known to King*
> *Nebuchadnezzar what will be in the latter days."*

> DANIEL 2:27-28

Those who put their trust in the Zodiac, the predictions of astrologers, or the "wisdom" of the horoscope are on shaky ground for sure. The Word says delving into these dark practices and listening to these deceptive voices first steals your peace of mind:

> *Hear the word which the Lord speaks to you, O*
> *house of Israel. Thus says the Lord: "Do not learn the*
> *way of the Gentiles; do not be dismayed at the signs*
> *of heaven, for the Gentiles are dismayed at them."*

> JEREMIAH 10:1-2

Then, these false prophecies lead to judgment:

> *You are wearied in the multitude of your counsels; let now the*
> *astrologers, the stargazers, and the monthly prognosticators*
> *stand up and save you from what shall come upon you.*
> *Behold, they shall be as stubble, the fire shall burn them;*
> *they shall not deliver themselves from the power of the flame.*

> ISAIAH 47:13-14

And finally, worshipping the heavens—the Sun, Moon, stars and signs within them—leads to death.

> *"At that time," says the Lord, "they shall bring out*
> *the bones of the kings of Judah, and the bones of its*
> *princes, and the bones of the priests, and the bones of the*
> *prophets, and the bones of the inhabitants of Jerusalem,*
> *out of their graves. They shall spread them before the*
> *sun and the moon and all the host of heaven, which they*
> *have loved and which they have served and after which*
> *they have walked, which they have sought and which*
> *they have worshiped. They shall not be gathered nor*
> *buried; they shall be like refuse on the face of the earth."*

JEREMIAH 8:1-2 NKJV

My friend, do not fear the signs in the heavens or Jesus' story in the stars that we are about to uncover, or recover! The devil comes to steal, kill and destroy, and he's used the Zodiac to accomplish this for far too long. It's time for the people of God to stop hiding from the Mazzaroth and the signs within it, and take back this life-giving revelation from the witches and New Age mystics. The signs in the heavens have always been, and will always be, the story of Jesus.

How the Book of the Heavens Works

The prophetic story of redemption that is told through the heavens is played out for us visually, dramatically, and progressively, and can only be learned through dedication to the Author Himself. This is how all prophetic things work. Let's unpack this a little bit.

Once you understand that the Word was written in the heavens before it was written in the Bible, you must begin to understand how to read it. Here are three important keys to understanding how to read the written language in the heavens:

1. It is prophetic

2. It is visual

3. It is rotational and progressive

It Is Prophetic

Prophetic things are deep for a reason; they have to be searched out. The Lord desires intimacy and relationship. That's why your interest and passion for knowing God through His creation in the night sky is a key qualifier for this prophetic revelation. The prophetic can't be taught. It must be caught!

> *It is the glory of God to conceal a matter, but*
> *the glory of kings is to search out a matter.*

PROVERBS 25:2 NKJV

You don't understand prophetic things unless you are committed to searching them out. This is what separates the merely curious from true seekers. Be a seeker. Act like a king and search out the matter.

On a more practical note, there are summer constellations and winter constellations. Some are very easy to recognize and some require some skill sets. At whatever level you want to read and interpret the signs of the heavens, there are some things you have to know. The first one—and a big one—is this:

The pictures match the names of the stars within the constellation.

The heavens declare the glory of God; and
the firmament shows His handiwork.

PSALM 19:1

The heavens are the broad spectrum and the individual constellations and stars are they rails this revelation runs on. God named the stars. Just like ours, their names are a testimony that tells a story.

Lift up your eyes on high, and see who has created
these things, who brings out their host by number; He
calls them all by name, by the greatness of His might
and the strength of His power; not one is missing.

ISAIAH 40:26

He counts the number of the stars; He calls them all by name.

PSALM 147:4

Like I said in the introduction, the ancient names of the stars can still be found today in both Arabic and Hebrew. They are named to give the details of the story. The prophetic numbers associated with stars also reveal details of the story. As part of God's design, they vary in light-years (distance) and in luminosity. These numbers have a role to play in the story as well. Search out the matter. In the Bible, not only are the words prophetic, how the words are written is also prophetic and must be fulfilled. Jesus said in Matthew 5:18,

For assuredly, I say to you, till heaven and
earth pass away, one jot or one tittle will by
no means pass from the law till all is fulfilled.

Just like that, not only does the message of the constellations prophesy Jesus our Redeemer, how they are placed from our perspective adds depth and meaning to the revelation.

It Is Visual

The signs in the heavens are prophetic pictures. Prophetic pictures are very symbolic. When God does prophetic things through pictures and still visuals, they have to be likened unto something else. Think of Jesus telling a parable. It's not hard, but the seeker has to be intentional. God has equipped us with a human brain that naturally connects the dots. When you look up at the night sky and see a constellation, you can't help but see the outline of an image. God made our brains just two days after He made the heavens for, among other things, prophetic signs for us to see and decode.

Then God said, "Let there be lights in the firmament
of the heavens to divide the day from the night; and let
them be for signs and seasons, and for days and years."

GENESIS 1:14

Since we are talking about connecting the dots, He has also given us the person of the Holy Spirit to help us find meaningful patterns and sound conclusions in otherwise meaningless noise. It is a scientific fact that predators are confused by patterns. It's why zebras have stripes. I think the difference the Holy Spirit makes within us separates us from brute beasts. It also causes us to see the patterns instead of being confused by them. God can engage our primitive brains with supernatural understanding through prophetic pictures in the stars. He has been broadcasting His deepest truths through the things He created.

For since the creation of the world His invisible
attributes are clearly seen, being understood by
the things that are made, even His eternal power
and Godhead, so that they are without excuse.

ROMANS 1:20

The Picture Didn't Fade

When I was a kid, critics of the Bible would point out that printed Bibles had only been in use for about 500 years. Prior to that, the scriptures were handwritten and every Bible was a copy made from a previous copy. Nobody had the original texts so there was no real way to know that the Bible wasn't full of errors, even full-scale additions. Then, some brilliant genius other than Al Gore invented the worldwide web. The Christian world began to learn about the Dead Sea Scrolls.

The Dead Sea Scrolls date 1,000 years prior to known manuscripts, yet the text shows no deviation. God has proven His Word. Just like that, the pictures God intended for us to see are remarkably intact despite millenniums of astrologers, mystical magi, New Age mystics, and demonic knuckleheads. Some of those pictures are messed up like Cancer the crab. The Jews considered crabs to be unclean vermin and that was not the original picture. However, the claws are still there and that's the main point of the picture as you will find out in a later chapter. Cancer is about the heart of God that will never let go—no matter what!

Another notable example is Ursa Major, also known as the Big Dipper. Both of those are aliases that I will explain later in the book, however I am amazed at how God has preserved His Word in the heavenly pictures throughout the cultures of the world. Bullinger wrote over 100 years ago:

No one can dispute the antiquity of the signs of the Zodiac, or of the constellations. No one can question the accuracy of the ancient star names which have come down to us, for they are still preserved in every good celestial atlas.

There are 88 constellations we see from our vantage point called Earth. Of these, there are 12 major constellations in the heavens that the Sun passes through. These are known as the "signs" of the Mazzaroth that act like 12 chapters of a book. There is a new chapter for every month of the year and surrounding all 12 signs are three constellations. These three constellations very often back up the main story of the sign. Sometimes, they also provide subplots and backstories as additional prophetic layers of God's amazing plan. So, the signs, constellations, and the names of the stars tell the story precisely, and in a very dramatic way.

It Is Progressive

>...luckily the camera does spin.

> MARK WATNEY from the movie, *The Martian*

There are 12 major signs that progressively rotate throughout the heavens. When we say they rotate, it means a new one comes up in the night sky every month and an old one goes down every month. There are 12 signs—one for every month. This story has been told from start to finish every year for millennia. I wrote a book called *Numbers that Preach*, and I like to talk about the number 12. It marks when God is in control of something. It's the number of His government He likes to use to show us He's ruling and reigning. That's why Jesus declared He could call on the power of 12 legions of angels (Matthew 26:53) during His ministry on Earth.

Now before I go any further, let me show you exactly how in control He was in 2 Kings 19:35 and Isaiah 37:36: One angel killed 185,000 Assyrians. Just one! Now Jesus said He could call down 12 legions and one legion is 6,000 angels. So, if you simply multiply that number by 12, you'll discover 12 legions of angels would be a minimum of 72,000 angels. This is the number of angels Jesus said was available to Him on the night of His arrest. When you multiply 72,000 angels with the ability to kill 185,000 soldiers, we find that there was enough combined strength at Jesus' disposal to have annihilated at least 13,320,000,000 souls. That is more people than have ever lived! Here are a few more 12s in scripture that prophetically speak of God's government, His sovereignty, and how He rules and reigns over it all:

- Jesus had 12 disciples. He set up the Church with the foundation of 12 teachable, yieldable men who would drop their plans and follow Him anywhere.

- The New Jerusalem has 12 gates and 12 foundations (Revelation 21:13-14).

- There are also 12 pearls and 12 angels associated with the New Jerusalem. The measurements of that "city" are seen as 12,000 furlongs, or stadia, while the wall will be 144 (12 x 12) cubits (Revelation 21:16-17).

- The first recorded words of Jesus were at the age of 12.

- There were 12 baskets of fragments left over when Jesus miraculously fed the crowd of people.

- There were 12 spies sent out by Moses in Numbers chapter 13.

- Elijah built an altar of 12 stones when he called fire down from Heaven on Mt. Carmel (1 Kings 18:31).

Here's the rub: The same God who designed the world to be 24,000 (12,000 x 2) miles around, also designed it to travel 1,600,000 (12 x 13,333) miles in one day as it orbits the Sun—which has a diameter of 864,000 (12 x 72,000) miles. He stamped the number twelve all over it as He did with the moon which orbits us, having a linear diameter of 1,260 (12 x 105) miles. That same God decided a day would have 24 (12 x 2) hours in it and 24 (12 x 2) time zones on that planet. The same God who designed those things, also designed in His written Word that John would notice the 24 elders who circle the throne of God nearly 1,600 years before the longitude problem was solved and anyone had a clue that 24 also circled the Earth. If you pay attention to the numbers, it is easy to see that the same

God who designed the world is the same God who designed the biblical picture of the heavenly throne room. That's why 60 (12 x 5) seconds make one minute and 60 minutes make 1 degree of longitude. That's why 60 minutes make one hour, 360 degrees (12 x 30) completes one circle, and it takes 3,600 seconds (12 x 300) to make one hour. He is saying that in every minute, of every day, in every time zone, "I am in control." As we say in Texas, "How 'bout them apples?"

When it comes to the sign of each month, it is not that you can see the sign in the heavens at night, but rather when the Sun is shining from within the constellation during the day. Nonetheless, whether you are going by day or by night, it is a progressive revelation being played out chapter by chapter, year after year. One part is revealed at a time. Prophetic revelation is always progressive (1 Corinthians 13:9). Prophetic things need to be developed; always building upon the last revelation and the last act of faith toward that revelation. You don't learn that Jesus is going to pay the price for your sin until you understand a price

must be paid. You don't understand a price must be paid until you understand that "the wages of sin is death."

Day unto day utters speech,
And night unto night reveals knowledge.

PSALM 19:2

Mystery Solved: The Beginning and the End

The story in the heavens is not only prophetically progressive, it is a rotating story. It is always the same with the exception of comets, planets, eclipses, and otherwise unscheduled events. This is why you need to know where the story starts and where it ends. Where does a kid jump on this merry-go-round? The Greeks and the astrologers have it wrong. They can study it, but they just can't get it because there is a blessing in getting it and they refuse the blessing because they deny the Creator.

Because, although they knew God, they did not glorify
Him as God, nor were thankful, but became futile in
their thoughts, and their foolish hearts were darkened.

ROMANS 1:21

The Greeks who created the Zodiac and peddle the horoscopes that control people's lives say it begins with Aries and ends with Pisces. That's not the way it was meant to be. Prophetic stories and timelines are discovered prophetically (1 Chronicles 12:32) and these jokers have no prophetic revelation because the Holy Spirit doesn't live within them. The grand drama of the heavens has begun with Virgo for thousands of recorded years. When you compare Virgo to the other eleven signs, this is only place it can start. The story of redemption unfolds with the promised Redeemer as the seed of the woman in Virgo, then progressively moves all the way to the Lion of the tribe of Judah coming back for His Bride in the sign of Leo. It starts in Genesis and ends in Revelation!

To prove this was His original intent, God has provided a testimony to preserve His Word that all the world knows about. It is called the Sphinx. Connected to the Great Pyramid, which is an ancient astral structure, the Sphinx is also known as one of the twelve ancient wonders of the world. The word *sphinx* means "bind together" or to "bind closely together." It is designed to show us where the story begins, ends, and begins again. The sphinx has the head of a woman and the body of a lion! It is screaming to all the world throughout all ages that the story begins with Virgo and ends at Leo. Bullinger tells us in *The Witness of the Stars* that at the giant Zodiac surrounding the Temple of Esneh in Egypt, a sphinx is actually placed between the signs of Virgo and Leo. Boom! There it is. Who can argue with the Sphinx?

A Room with a View

Just like the mobile over a baby's crib, space has always captured the human imagination. That's the point. King Jesus created the stars, planets, and heavens above to grab our attention and arouse our curiosity. They speak to us, don't they? Yes, The Word is the master communicator who spoke every star, planet, solar system and galaxy into just the right place to tell a story–His story–to generations and generations of people right here on what the Bible calls "the firmament." This, my friend, is where the revelation truly begins.

Laying the Groundwork

The Bible has plenty to say about foundations and building upon the rock. In fact, that's what most thinking people would tell you the word *firmament* means—a bunch of rocks. They would say the firmament is the firm ground beneath our feet, as opposed to oceans, seas, and heavens. That's because they only consider Genesis 1:6. Let's keep reading and look at firmament in context of God's Word:

> *Then God said, "Let there be a firmament in the midst of the waters, and let it divide the waters from the waters." Thus God made the firmament, and divided the waters which were under the firmament from the waters which were above the firmament; and it was so. And God called the firmament Heaven. So the evening and the morning were the second day.*

> GENESIS 1:6-8

BOOM! Right there we find the firmament is not only on Earth in the midst of the waters, but also in the heavens. What does that mean? It's a word on our outlook, frame of reference, and point of view. Firmament literally means "from our perspective on earth" or how humans view the universe from this floating rock we call planet Earth.

"We" are here

Think about it. Our solar system has been uniquely and carefully placed to give us a vantage point to see "out" of our galaxy and observe the universe with a breathtakingly clear view of other galaxies and amazing phenomena. The Word who later became flesh and dwelt among us created the universe to be seen and understood from our perspective. While that is incredible in itself, it is also deeply personal. Why would God Almighty care how we view the cosmos? Because He wants us to see Him in it and hear His voice. He wants us to see His hand of goodness at work. He is speaking a great big story of love, loss, and redemption for those curious enough to wonder "where do I fit in among all this grand design?"

Then God said, "Let there be lights in the firmament of the heavens to divide the day from the night; and let them be for signs and seasons, and for days and years; and let them be for lights in the firmament of the heavens to give light on the earth"; and it was so.

GENESIS 1:14-15

The firmament is set so we can observe and understand the signs and seasons, or times. How do I know Earth is uniquely placed on an outer arm of a spiral galaxy in a position to discern the handwriting of God on the walls of Heaven? There are at least four examples I can give you of galactic wonders that are only wonders from where you and I stand here on the third rock from the Sun.

Example 1:
The Analemma

Because of Earth's exact 23.5 degree tilt and its slightly elliptical orbit, the Sun makes a figure-eight pattern in the sky called the analemma over the course of a year. If you were to take a photograph from the same exact location at the same exact time every day for a year and overlap the images, you would see something so perfect and constant, it could not be accidental or random chance—a remnant from a giant cosmic explosion.

In God's mathematical lingo, the number eight is all about new beginnings and the Word says God's mercies are new every morning! Lay that eight on its side and God is speaking a great big word on His eternal nature and Godhead.

> *For thus says the High and Lofty One Who inhabits eternity, whose name is Holy: "I dwell in the high and holy place, with him who has a contrite and humble spirit, to revive the spirit of the humble, and to revive the heart of the contrite ones."*

ISAIAH 57:15

There you have it. Everything is perfectly set in place for you and I to see the promise of the number eight in the analemma. Astronomers say the chances of this phemomenon being seen from anywhere else in the universe are impossible.

Example 2:
Polaris, the North Star

Polaris is not the brightest star in the heavens, but it is the center of our "universe" as it is seen as fixed in the sky. It never moves from our perspective. All other heavenly bodies revolve around it (Colossians 1:17). Prophetically, it represents Jesus Himself

who was not the tallest, most handsome guy around, but He is the center of all things.

> *For He shall grow up before Him as a tender*
> *plant, and as a root out of dry ground. He has*
> *no form or comeliness; And when we see Him,*
> *There is no beauty that we should desire Him.*

ISAIAH 53:2

In the tail of the "Little Bear" Ursa Minor, aka the Little Dipper, Polaris is actually a triple star, which speaks a word on the Trinity of Father, Son and Holy Spirit. Because Polaris is the 50th-brightest star in the heavens, God's prophetic number for jubilee fulfilled, you and I have to be looking for Polaris to find it—just like Jesus said to seek Him and you will find Him. Like the North Star, if you find Jesus, you will never be lost again because according to Isaiah 14:13, 40:22, and Psalm

89:11-12, the North is the location of God's throne. It's literally the way home!

While that is all crazy cool information, what's real is this is only possible from our unique perspective on Earth.

Example 3:
The Whirlpool Galaxy

At 23.16 light-years from Earth, the Whirlpool Galaxy is our closest neighbor. It is also known as Messier 51. Named after the man who discovered it, Messier means "Harvest Master" in French. So, what is the big deal about the Whirlpool Galaxy and why is it sitting like giant stop sign in space from our firmament? What does God want us to see?

Well, doing exactly like I would if I had a giant radio telescope, astronomers pointed that instrument directly at the center of the Whirlpool Galaxy and what did they find?

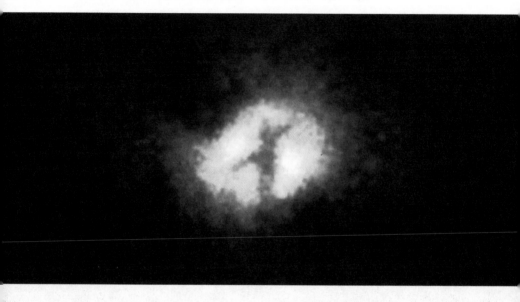

The scientific community calls this "The X-Structure" but to any drop-dead, sold-out Jesus freak, it looks like a cross. By the way, "X" stands for "cristos" or "Christ" in Greek—the Lord of the Harvest (Matthew 9:38; Luke 10:2). The redemption of mankind was literally written in the stars above just waiting for us to discover it.

Example 4:
Eclipses

This will blow your mind. Mathematically, Earth is the only place in the universe a full solar and lunar eclipse is possible. Why? The sun is exactly 400 times larger than the moon and exactly 400 times farther away from our planet. This makes them appear to be the same size from our firmament. In a solar eclipse where the Sun is blotted out, the Moon moves between the Earth and Sun. In a lunar eclipse where the moon turns dark or red, the Earth comes between the Sun and Moon, causing the Earth's shadow to create a perfect "blackout" from our perspective. According to astronomers, the odds that this is possible in other planetary systems are astronomical.

So, it's very true that perspective is everything! God Almighty has proven His sovereignty through the mathematical precision needed to make these amazing heavenly happenings possible for us to see day after day, night after night. Now that we have set the stage, so to speak, let's consider the story itself—and it's epic!

The Drama Begins

The story in the stars is written in three acts. First, we have to understand that God is going to make and keep an impossible promise: redemption for the sin of all mankind for all time.

Act One

Virgo, Libra, Scorpio, Sagittarius

Together, these four signs represent the period of the Old Testament right up to the cross and resurrection of Christ. We learn the body of Christ, the Church, will receive power and act as His ambassadors on Earth.

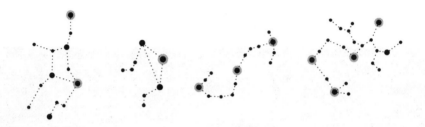

Act Two (The Sea)

Capricorn, Aquarius, Pisces, Aries

These four "water signs" represent the period of time between the ascension of Jesus into Heaven in the book of Acts until the rapture of the Church in Revelation chapter four. We learn Jesus Christ will come back again and bring His people back to Jerusalem, Israel, to rule and reign over all nations.

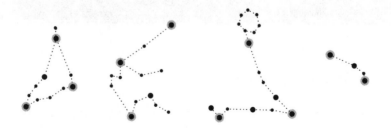

Act Three

Taurus, Gemini, Cancer, Leo

Representing the return of Jesus Christ, these four signs cover the time period from Revelation chapter 23 into eternity future. This is the part of your Bible which starts with Jesus coming back to whoop up on His enemies, triumph over evil, set up a new Kingdom on Earth where He can "tabernacle" with mankind and we live with Him for millennia.

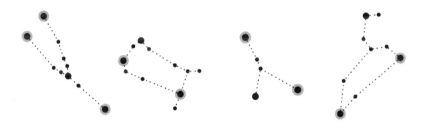

In short, Act one is before the resurrection of Jesus. Act two is after the resurrection of Jesus and Act three is after the return of Jesus, or the prophesied "Second Coming."

Summary

- Before the Bible was written in the form of a book, it was written in the stars. God programmed human beings in ancient days to look up and recognize the patterns in the heavens as prophetic images revealing His heart and how He would carry out His plan through a Messiah/Redeemer.

- God named all the stars and to this day, they have ancient Arabic and Hebrew names. The names of the stars give the detail, a lot like adding bullet points to an idea or headline to a news article.

- A sign is a constellation the Sun passes through. There are 12 major signs and 36 minor constellations which support the 12 and bring depth to the story. Every month, a new prophetic sign rises above the horizon. At the end of the year the entire story has been told. It is a progressive revelation that begins with Virgo the Virgin and ends with Leo, the Lion of the tribe of Judah, coming back the same way the Bible describes in Revelation. The story is the same as the Bible because the Author of the Bible and the Creator of the universe is the same person.

- We are not talking about the Zodiac, which witches and New Age mystics have used to deceive and control millions of people. The revelation of the story of Jesus being written in the stars before it was written in the heavens is well known and documented in scripture (the Mazzaroth) as well as in Jewish culture. Ancient star names support this universal telling of the story, and the Egyptian sphinx also testifies to the reality of the "book of the heavens." This book takes back what the enemy has stolen and twisted so this final generation will see the truth of Jesus in the night sky.

- The key to understanding the revelation of *Looking Up* lies in the firmament. While many believe this means "firm or solid ground," the firmament actually means "from our perspective on earth." All of the universe was created to be seen and understood from our vantage point on Earth. This points to a very loving God who wants to communicate a story—His story—to His creation across the world and for all time.

Lift up your eyes on high,
And see who has created these things,
Who brings out their host by number;
He calls them all by name,
By the greatness of His might
And the strength of His power;
Not one is missing.

ISAIAH 40:26

CHAPTER

TWO

This Is What It Says

The story of redemption declared
and made known

S ome of my greatest heroes have been amazing storytellers, like the mighty Davey Crockett and President Abraham Lincoln. I think it is a godly quality because God Himself is the inventor of compelling storytelling. We see a tiny glimpse of Him through the genius of Spielberg and Shakespeare, but they have nothing on Him. He is the greatest of all authors and communicators. Nobody's sold more books than the Bible, and no one's stories have changed the world like those of the Lord Jesus Christ.

In any good story, there are three basic parts that men have learned are essential to dramatic splendor. I am convinced that people learned this through the stories in the heavens and it became the standard of good storytelling in every culture throughout the world.

Awesome Storytelling 101 basically works like this:

1. Introduce a worthy hero with a massive goal.

2. Plunge the hero into chaos, then force the hero to fight for freedom.

3. Show how the hero overcomes.

In the Story of the Heavens, the Hero is Jesus

Some examples of Jesus as the Hero of the heavens are:

- He's "The Branch" promised in Virgo, who will be born of a virgin (Jeremiah 33:15, Isaiah 7:14).

- He's the double-natured conqueror, Sagittarius the Archer, aiming at the heart of death itself (Revelation 6:2).

- He's the Glorious King who pours out His water of life in Aquarius (Numbers 24:7).

- He is the Lion of the tribe of Judah whose feet stomp the devil in Leo (the Lion) and Hydra (the Serpent) (Amos 3:4, Amos 3:8).

In this epic account, our hero Jesus battles on our behalf. Remember, this drama which plays out and repeats every twelve months in the heavens is God's plan of redemption and restoration for all of us! This is the story He wants known. So consequently:

- Jesus is the light of the world in Orion with truth in His belt, setting His bride upright and removing death from the picture (John 8:12, 1 Corinthians 15:55).

- He is the one who balances the scales of Libra by declaring a price will be paid for the redemption of His people (Psalm 49:7, Isaiah 40:12, Daniel 5:27).

- Jesus is the goat of atonement slain for the redeemed in Capricorn (Leviticus 10:16,17).

Here's where you and I come into the story. In the heavenly drama, Jesus overcomes and shares that with us. Because of His victory over sin, death, and hell, we can become overcomers just like Him. His victory is our victory!

In the Story of the Heavens, Jesus Is the Conquering Hero Who Causes His People to Overcome

- Jesus causes His people to multiply and to be teeming with life in Pisces the Fish (Genesis 48:15-16).

- He is the Living Lamb who was slain, but now ascending as King in Aries the Lamb (Revelation 5:12).

- He is the God of breakthrough who cannot be stopped in Taurus the Bull (Micah 2:13).

- He is the One who gives His nature, His life and His righteousness to the ones He loves in Gemini the Twins (Jeremiah 23:5-6).

We could go on, and of course, we will as we look at all of the signs individually. But know this: the story in the heavens is all about God's great vengeance upon the thing that separated us from Him and His great love. It is the story of restoration for those of us who are His.

> *For the wrath of God is revealed from heaven against all ungodliness and unrighteousness of men, who suppress the truth in unrighteousness.*
>
> ROMANS 1:18

He is shown in the heavens as the fixer of the problem and the answer to the dilemma. That is who He is and how He wants to be known. It's important to Him that we see Him this way. So let's roll the heavenly tape and cause the sky to pass before us beginning at Virgo and ending at Leo. Let's see what the story of the heavens actually says. It takes a whole year for this story to play out, and a lifetime to investigate the subplots, backstory and supporting characters. Let's just lay out the story in a brief description, according to the 12 major signs, or chapters, in the heavens and the three constellations within each sign.

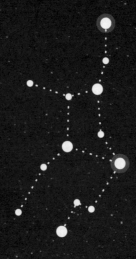

–SIGN 1–

VIRGO THE VIRGIN

The three constellations within the sign:
COMA (The Woman and Child)
CENTAURUS (The Centaur)
BOOTES (The Coming One)

WHAT THE FIRST PART
OF THE STORY TELLS US

Sin has happened. People need to be delivered and redeemed. God promises to send a Messiah through a virgin woman. He will be a "righteous branch" and a "conquering King." He will be both 100 percent human and 100 percent God at the same time. He will be both the desire of all nations and a despised sin offering. His offering will be our ransom and once He has died and resurrected, He will come to Earth again.

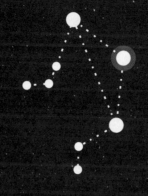

−SIGN 2−

LIBRA THE SCALES

The three constellations within the sign:
CRUX (The Cross)
LUPUS or VICTIMA (The Victim)
CORONA (The Crown)

WHAT THE SECOND PART
OF THE STORY TELLS US

The law is introduced. A price must be paid. The blood at first will cover sin, then it will completely redeem. Atonement must be produced and He will do it on a cross! He will lay down His life and take on what all of His people should be victimized by: sin. He will be surrounded by dogs and treated like a dog. It is a terrible, horrible price that must be paid, but He will do it! He will do this for the joy that is set before Him. He will do this thing that no other can do, and will not remain defeated, but be exalted as the greatest King ever.

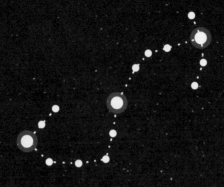

–SIGN 3–

SCORPIO THE SCORPION

The three constellations within the sign:
SERPENS (The Snake)
OPHIUCHUS (The Snake Handler)
HERCULES (The Mighty One)

WHAT THE THIRD PART
OF THE STORY TELLS US

There is a great war against the powers of darkness and death itself! Though many have been wounded, a crushing blow to the enemy is coming! Though many battles have been lost, the war will be won! The serpent will not get the crown. Dominion belongs to our mighty King and to those of His Kingdom. It's an ugly battle. Death will not have the victory, and the struggle will be worth it.

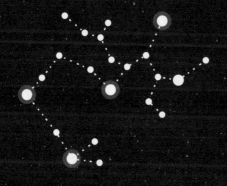

–SIGN 4–

SAGITTARIUS THE ARCHER

The three constellations within the sign:

LYRA (The Harp)

ARA (The Altar)

DRACO (The Dragon)

WHAT THE FOURTH PART
OF THE STORY TELLS US

The power and glory of the conquering Prince will be awesome! We will see Him both as God and as a human being who is the very apex of all humanity. His light is not to be compared with the enemy's darkness. We will give praise to our utmost and sing to our highest at His coming. He will have His great day of vengeance and will cast the dragon into the lake of fire. The enemy will be destroyed and that day will be the greatest of all days.

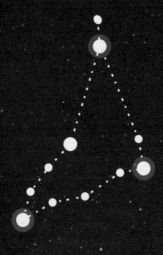

–SIGN 5–

CAPRICORN THE SEA GOAT

The three constellations within the sign:
SAGITTA (The Arrow)
AQUILA (The Eagle)
DELPHINUS (The Dolphin)

WHAT THE FIFTH PART
OF THE STORY TELLS US

The story of redemption is not only about the sacrifice, but about the ones He has redeemed. The Messiah will die and out of Him will come a great multitude of redeemed people. God's great deliverance will shoot forth and after He is wounded unto death, He will rise again and come busting out of the grave, victorious upon the behalf of the redeemed!

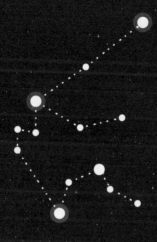

–SIGN 6–

AQUARIUS THE WATER BEARER

The three constellations within the sign:
PISCIS AUSTRALIS (The Southern Fish)
PEGASUS (The Winged Horse)
CYGNUS (The Swan)

WHAT THE SIXTH PART
OF THE STORY TELLS US

After His resurrection, He will pour out His Holy Spirit upon His redeemed and the whole earth will be blessed! It will be like pouring water out into a dry place. His people will perform miracles and they shall be as a well springing up. This blessing will come suddenly and will remain until the Messiah returns.

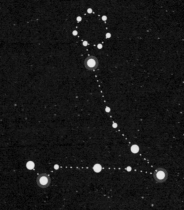

–SIGN 7–

PISCES THE FISH

The three constellations within the sign:
THE BAND (Of Covenant)
ANDROMEDA (The Chained Woman)
CEPHEUS (The Crowned King)

WHAT THE SEVENTH PART
OF THE STORY TELLS US

The multiplied seed of Abraham will be like the sands of the sea and the stars of Heaven. The people of God will be blessed and multiply through covenant. The bride of the King is in desperate need of a Savior, but the King is coming!

–SIGN 8–

ARIES THE RAM

The three constellations within the sign:

CASSIOPEIA (The Enthroned Woman)

CETUS (The Sea Monster)

PERSEUS (The Breaker)

WHAT THE EIGHTH PART
OF THE STORY TELLS US

The Lamb who was slain is worthy to receive power and honor as King. He will make His bride righteous, bind the enemy, and remove all power and authority from the devil. His Kingdom will come and His will be done on earth as it is in Heaven.

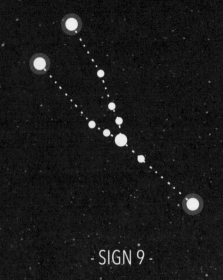

- SIGN 9 -

TAURUS THE BULL

The three constellations within the sign:
ORION (The Coming Prince)
ERIDANUS (The River of Fire)
AURIGA (The Shepherd)

WHAT THE NINTH PART
OF THE STORY TELLS US

When the Messiah returns, He will be unstoppable and He is coming to rule. He was wounded before, but He will not be this time. He is the Prince of Peace and the most glorious in all of Heaven. He is the Light of the World and He stands upon the enemy—crushing him with feet of judgment. He will pour out His wrath like a river of fire and His judgment is set. He brings the sheep of His flock and the bride of His chamber back safely with Him.

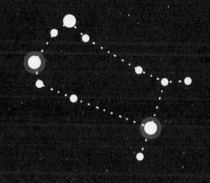

–SIGN 10–

GEMINI THE TWINS

The three constellations within the sign:
LEPUS (The Hare), THE ENEMY
CANIS MAJOR (The Dog) or SIRIUS (The Prince)
CANIS MINOR (The Second Dog)

WHAT THE TENTH PART
OF THE STORY TELLS US

God and man will dwell together in perfect harmony. The lion will lay down with the lamb, The One who was slain and hated will rule and reign as beloved and honored. A time of peace and rest will come after the enemy is trodden underfoot. The King of Kings and sire of all will rule as Prince of Peace and as the Redeemer of all mankind.

–SIGN 11–

CANCER THE CRAB

The three constellations within the sign:
URSA MINOR (The Little Bear)
URSA MAJOR (The Great Bear)
ARGO (The Ship)

WHAT THE ELEVENTH PART
OF THE STORY TELLS US

The Messiah's redemption will encircle His people and He will never let go of them. His people are a precious possession to Him and He has bought them with a price—His blood. He has redeemed and ransomed them and no one can snatch them out of His hand or from out of His possession. They will journey through life and progressively travel until they are each safely home.

–SIGN 12–

LEO THE LION

The three constellations within the sign:
HYDRA (The Destroyed Serpent)
CRATER (The Cup of Wrath Being Poured Out)
CORVUS (The Bird of Prey)

WHAT THE TWELFTH PART
OF THE STORY TELLS US

The Lion of the Tribe of Judah will come back and utterly destroy the enemy. He will pour out His wrath and trod all enemies underfoot. He will put down the enemy as a Warrior King. He will dish out His judgment and fury upon the serpent, and afterward, the birds of the air will feast upon the armies of the enemy. He shall roar on high and descend from Heaven with a mighty shout. Then, He will rule and reign forever and ever.

This is the same story of redemption as told from the Redeemer Himself. It is progressively revealed throughout the centuries through the writers of the Bible. It is also the same story revealed by the Author of the heavens and progressively told from sign to sign and from night unto night.

The heavens declare the glory of God;
And the firmament shows His handiwork.
Day unto day utters speech,
And night unto night reveals knowledge.

PSALM 19:1-2

The Author of the Bible and the signs of the heavens is the same. The Hero and Messiah of the redemption story are the same. Nothing is left out.

Lift up your eyes on high, And
see who has created these things,
Who brings out their host by number; He calls
them all by name, By the greatness of His might,
And the strength of His power; Not one is missing.

ISAIAH 40:26

...looking unto Jesus, the author and finisher of
our faith, who for the joy that was set before Him
endured the cross, despising the shame, and has
sat down at the right hand of the throne of God.

HEBREWS 12:2

Simply summing it up in the correct order of rotation:

- VIRGO: There is a Messiah coming.
- LIBRA: He will be a Redeemer.
- SCORPIO: There will be a war and He will die.
- SAGITTARIUS: He will resurrect and conquer death.
- CAPRICORN: From His death, a living people will be born.
- AQUARIUS: He will pour out His Spirit upon them all.
- PISCES: His people will multiply and bless the earth.
- ARIES: His Kingdom will come and His will be done.
- TAURUS: He will return with His people on behalf of Israel.
- GEMINI: His people will be just like Him.
- CANCER: He will never let go of them as His possession.
- LEO: He will rule and reign supreme throughout the universe.

This is the story God wants the whole world to know and it is played out in dramatic splendor before all of us.

The heavens declare the glory of God;
And the firmament shows His handiwork.
Day unto day utters speech,
And night unto night reveals knowledge.
There is no speech nor language
Where their voice is not heard.

PSALM 19:1-3

For the word of the Lord is right,
And all His work is done in truth.
He loves righteousness and justice;
The earth is full of the goodness of the Lord.
By the word of the Lord, the heavens were made,
And all the host of them by the breath of His mouth.

PSALM 33:4-6

THREE

The Drama Unfolds in 12 Acts

A closer look at things Kingdom and
things Astro through all 12 signs

Can you bind the cluster of the Pleiades,
Or loose the belt of Orion?
Can you bring out Mazzaroth in its season?
Or can you guide the Great Bear with its cubs?
Do you know the ordinances of the heavens?
Can you set their dominion over the earth?

JOB 38:31-33

—SIGN 1—

VIRGO THE VIRGIN

The Prophetic Promise: The Virgin birth of the Redeemer, the Lord Jesus Christ.

*"Behold, the virgin shall be with child, and
bear a Son, and they shall call His name
Immanuel," which is translated, "God with us."*

MATTHEW 1:23

The story in the heavens starts out the same as the account in the Bible because both have the same Author. Remember, the story is the prophecy of the Messiah's redemption of mankind—the creation He, along with the Father and Holy Spirit, breathed their Spirit into—making us in Their amazing image. That is a revelation we'll be unpacking even into eternity! With that said, the first time we see the very beginning of that story, he Bible uses prophecy as God spoke to the devil in the first book of the Bible.

*And I will put enmity between you and the woman,
and between your seed and her Seed; He shall
bruise your head, and you shall bruise His heel.*

GENESIS 3:15

The answer to the problem of separation through sin would come from a woman, which is such redemption as the original fall of mankind started with a woman. Eve gets a really bad rap, but she wasn't alone in that Garden. She had no guile. She didn't understand what a lie was or how to understand deception. Could Adam have stepped in? We don't know. We just know his bite into the forbidden cost you and I everything. But God is not surprised. He has a solution and it's a child. In a progressive and prophetic revelation, we learn this child is no ordinary baby. He is divine. The seed He comes from is not of human origin. This child is to be born of a woman and she is a virgin.

> *Then he said, "Hear now, O house of David! Is it a*
> *small thing for you to weary men, but will you weary*
> *my God also? Therefore the Lord Himself will give*
> *you a sign: Behold, the virgin shall conceive and*
> *bear a Son, and shall call His name Immanuel."*

ISAIAH 7:13

The first sign given of the Messiah was that a human would be born of a virgin. It makes sense that the first sign in the order of the heavens would be Virgo the Virgin. In star maps, Virgo is represented as a woman with a branch in her right hand, and ears of corn in her left hand. She is a virgin with "seed," and it is impossible for a virgin woman to have seed because women don't carry seed. Men carry seed and women carry eggs. She's fertile, she's a virgin, she carries seed, and she is about to produce a harvest. This glorious sign doesn't just speak of the virgin, but the miraculous birth of the bringer of redemption.

Looking Up

The brightest star in Virgo the Virgin is known to us as Spica. It is the 15th brightest star in our view of the night sky. The Greeks didn't have any respect for its original name so in Latin, Spica means something like "head of wheat," "ear of grain," or more likely "corn." Even this name speaks of the harvest her child would bring, and again, it's all about the seed. Jesus is the LORD of the harvest. Before that was ever in the Bible, it was prophesied in the heavens.

Now He who supplies seed to the sower and bread
for food will supply and multiply your seed for
sowing and increase the harvest of your righteousness.

2 CORINTHIANS 9:10 ESV

Therefore pray the Lord of the harvest
to send out laborers into His harvest.

MATTHEW 9:38

The ancient name in all the old star maps is connected to the Hebrew word *tsemech*. In Arabic, it is Al Zimach, which means "the branch." This star is in the ear of corn which she holds in her left hand. This is the prophetic name of the seed of the virgin woman: The Branch. Now this prophetic name "branch" is seen all over the heavens, and consequently, in at least four biblical prophecies about the coming of the Messiah. In a lot of pictures of Virgo, she is actually seen holding a branch. The branch that Mary held was a child, and He was a divine seed who was foretold through the constellation Virgo.

Behold I will bring forth my servant, the BRANCH.

ZECHARIAH 3:8 KJV

Then speak to him, saying, "Thus says the Lord
of hosts, saying: 'Behold, the Man whose name is
the BRANCH! From His place He shall branch
out, and He shall build the temple of the Lord.'"

ZECHARIAH 6:12

There shall come forth a Rod from the stem of
Jesse, and a Branch shall grow out of his roots.

ISAIAH 11:1

Before that verse was written in the Bible, it was written in the heavens. Just like that, the next brightest star in Virgo is called Zavijaveh, which means "the gloriously beautiful." Hundreds of years before the Messiah entered the scene, the prophet Isaiah not only named Him "the Branch" twice (see verse 11:1 above), he called Him "beautiful."

In that day the Branch of the Lord shall be beautiful
and glorious; and the fruit of the earth shall be excellent
and appealing for those of Israel who have escaped.
In that day the Branch of the Lord shall be beautiful
and glorious; And the fruit of the earth shall be excellent
and appealing for those of Israel who have escaped.

ISAIAH 4:2

Your eyes will see the King in His beauty;
They will behold a far-distant land.

ISAIAH 33:17

The story continues with five more prophetic star names that I challenge you to look into for yourself. I have provided the scripture references. Do you have the honor of a king to search out the matter?

Names of other stars in this sign are:

- Al Mureddin, which means "who shall come down" (Psalm 72:8)

- Vindemiatrix, which means "the son, or branch, who cometh"
- Subilah, which means "he who carries" (Isaiah 46:4)
- Al Azal, which means "the Branch" (Isaiah 18:5)
- Subilon, which means "a spike of corn" (Isaiah 17:5)

Star Party

- Virgo is a congested constellation with 26 known exo-planets— planets outside of the solar system—orbiting around 20 stars, and at least a dozen Messier objects. Messier objects include galaxies, nebulae, and star clusters, catalogued by 18th Century French astronomer Charles Messier. He is worth looking into. It is interesting to note the name Messier literally means "Harvest Master" and he is the man who has mapped out our modern night sky!

- Virgo is the largest constellation of the Zodiac.

- Look for Spica—Virgo's brightest star and 15th overall in the night sky—to be at its highest point in the sky at mid-May around 10 p.m. (11 p.m. Daylight Savings Time), and in mid-June at about 8 p.m. (9 p.m. Daylight Savings Time).

- One of the cool ways you can find Spica is to follow the handle of the Big Dipper over to Arcturus, then keep going to Spica. The old saying that goes with this is, "Arc to Arcturus and speed on to Spica."

- Spica is 250 light-years from Earth and is one of the closest stars to our Sun. It is a blue giant star and Beta Cephei-type variable star. Spica is light blue because it is super-hot and one of the hottest things you'll ever see. Spica's surface is estimated at 40,000 degrees Fahrenheit. That is hotter than an arc welder.

- This star is actually a double star (called a binary star system). They orbit each other every four days. They are super close to each other.

The Heavens Declare the Glory of God.

–SIGN 2–

LIBRA THE SCALES

The Prophetic Promise: The Messiah Would Pay the Terrible Price Required for Our Redemption.

For the redemption of their souls is costly...

PSALM 49:8

Therefore take heed to yourselves and to all the flock, among which the Holy Spirit has made you overseers, to shepherd the church of God which He purchased with His own blood.

ACTS 20:28

As we move into the second part of this progressive revelation, keep in mind that we are still in the early stages of the dramatic story. There are certain precepts that must be known before we continue. Now we come to Libra, the scales, and are confronted with the debt that must be paid. Our God is a God of justice, and a great injustice has been done to His sons and daughters. They are deep in debt with no way to make the payment. When we are talking about Heaven's scales of justice, we are talking about righteous scales and they tell the truth.

Dishonest scales are an abomination to the Lord...

PROVERBS 11:1

Redemption is a payment for a legal debt. A price must be paid for the redemption of mankind because they cannot pay it themselves. Most are born into the debt of sin, death, and hell and have no way to balance the account. A redeemer is needed.

*TEKEL: You have been weighed in
the balances, and found wanting....*

DANIEL 5:27

The weight of our sin; this is the picture we have in the second sign. Not only is our debt really bad news, it's impossible for us to post our own bail. We are doomed forever in an eternal prison without a Messiah/Redeemer.

*None of them can by any means redeem his
brother, nor give to God a ransom for him....*

PSALM 49:7

Because the hero of our story is the central figure in every sign, we have great hope. The good news is that this is the story of how we are redeemed by the only person who ever could pay our penalty. This story is the first prophetic revelation of Jesus Christ.

...who gave Himself a ransom for all.

1 TIMOTHY 2:6

Looking Up

Have you ever looked at the price tag of something you really wanted and knew there was no way you could afford it? This is parable of seeing the sign of Libra. How long can you stand in the darkness looking up at these heavenly scales, and contemplate how we have missed the mark? How many centuries have the Jews contemplated the law and the sacrifice of atonement?

To stand and stare at a scale, a device that measures the weight of justice, can be a scary thing if you always come up short because there is no way to pay the debt. Can anyone pay this price? Only one. We have already been introduced to Him the previous month in the sign of Virgo. He is the seed of the woman. He is the one born of a virgin—the coming Branch.

The three minor constellations which go with the second sign can be no greater billboard pointing to who He is and how He would accomplish paying the price. Crux, the Cross, tells us the manner of his sacrifice on a Roman cross and Lupus, or Victima, the Victim prophesies He will remain dead three days. The constellation Corona, or Crown, tells us He will rise again and overcome everything, being victorious over death. The second sign given of the Messiah would be that He was coming to pay the price, personally.

Libra is represented as a two-sided scale and is a constellation with 51 stars traditionally represented in it. It's not a bright constellation, but it has several bright stars in it that form a triangle. Libra represents the law. Libra is the wages of sin, and it is the bill that Jesus proclaimed was paid in full at the cross when He said, "It is finished!" (John 19:30).

The ancient Hebrew name for this constellation is Mozanaim, which means "weighed in the balance" or "the weighing scales." In Arabic, it is called Al Zubena, which means "redemption." The brightest star is Zuben al Genubi, which means "the purchase" or "price which is deficient." It is easy for me to remember because it kind of rhymes with Obi Wan Kenobi. The other bright star in this constellation also sounds like a Jedi master: its name is Zubinalchemali, which means "the price which covers." This is the testimony of Jesus as described in Revelation.

And they sang a new song, saying: "You are worthy
to take the scroll, and to open its seals; For You were
slain, and have redeemed us to God by Your blood out
of every tribe and tongue and people and nation....."

REVELATION 5:9

The Greeks thought Libra to be the same as the constellation Scorpio. They said the two bright stars of Libra were the claws of the scorpion. No, they are not the same, but the scales and the scorpion do go together: the wages of sin (the message in Libra) is death (Scorpio).

For the wages of sin is death, but the gift of
God is eternal life in Christ Jesus our Lord.

ROMANS 6:23

Before that was written in the Bible, it was written in the heavens–with these two constellations together–because the Author is the same.

Star Party

- Libra is a fairly small, dim constellation with no very bright stars.

- Located in the northern hemisphere, Libra can be seen from April to July.

- Zubeneschamali (remember, it sounds like Obi Wan Kenobi), is a blue dwarf with a magnitude of 2.7 and is the constellation's brightest star. Revelation 2:7 says *"He who has an ear, let him hear what the Spirit says to the churches. To him who overcomes I will give to eat from the tree of life, which is in the midst of the Paradise of God."*

- Zubeneschamali is thought to be 160 light-years away. It is the only star to appear green to the naked eye. In Strong's Hebrew Concordance, 160 is related to the word "ahabah" which means "love." This makes sense as the number 16 is related to the love of God through the 16 traits of the love of God in 1 Corinthians 13. It was His love for us that caused Him to pay the ultimate price for our redemption.

- Libra is home to the star Gliese 581, which has a planetary system consisting of at least six planets. It has the first extrasolar planet ever discovered, which was a game-changer for astronomers. The earth-like planet, orbiting inside the habital zone of the star, was found in 2007. Another planet orbiting Gliese 581, is the smallest mass extrasolar planet discovered orbiting a normal star. In Strong's Greek Concordance, the number 581 is related to the word "apoginomai" which means "to be away, be removed from, depart life, or die." This word can be found in 1 Peter 2:24 *who Himself bore our sins in His own body on the tree, that we, having died to sins, might live for righteousness—by whose stripes you were healed.* Didn't I tell you the numbers associated with each sign support and also help tell the story?

The Heavens Declare the Glory of God.

-

–SIGN 3–

SCORPIO THE SCORPION

The Prophetic Promise: Our Messiah/ Redeemer Will War against Death on Our Behalf.

But God commended his love toward us, in that, while we were yet sinners, Christ died for us.

ROMANS 5:8 KJV

There is going to be a war! In scene three of our 12-part drama in the heavens, we come to the beautiful but deadly Scorpio. Like the proverbial woman in the red dress, she can't be ignored and our attraction to her could be deadly. Strung across the summer night sky, Scorpio is by far the largest and southernmost of all our southern constellations. This is the enemy that must be defeated. The giant that must be slain. This is the sign associated with Christ's warfare against death. The scorpion represents death itself. Not only is Scorpio the enemy, it represents the promise that Christ will come to destroy the works of the devil and bring life instead of death.

O death, where is thy sting? O grave, where is thy victory?

1 CORINTHIANS 15:55 KJV

In the first sign, we learn the Messiah will be the seed of a virgin woman, fully God and fully human. In the second sign, we learn the Messiah will pay the ransom for many and will pay the price only a divine Redeemer can. In this third sign, we discover the Messiah will be a mighty warrior who will confront the enemy and slap death in the face for all of us! He will defeat the dragon by going into the jaws of the dragon itself. Jesus will win the war over death by dying!

Scorpio is seen as a larger-than-life scorpion with a bright red heart and a powerful stinger. Its claws are almost touching the scales of Libra. Directly over the stinger is the foot of the man in the constellation Ophiucus—the one who is also battling a serpent. This and the surrounding constellations are all about warfare—the intent of King Jesus to utterly defeat death, hell, and the grave.

Looking Up

The brightest star in Scorpio is one of the brightest in all the heavens. Antares is the heart of the scorpion, and it dramatically shines blood red. The name of the star means "wounding." This is prophetic of the Messiah being wounded.

> *But He was wounded for our transgressions, He was*
> *bruised for our iniquities; The chastisement for our*
> *peace was upon Him, and by His stripes we are healed.*

> Isaiah 53:5

Since Antares is a red super giant, its dramatic color tells us that it is cooling down and its time is almost over. The different colors of the stars tell us where they are in a timeline, similar to any kind of flame. At one time, Antares was white hot. Now, its color is announcing its days are numbered and the number is short. Jesus is going to die, but He will not stay dead. What is soon approaching is pronounced in 1 Corinthians 15:53-55:

> *For this corruptible must put on incorruption, and this*
> *mortal must put on immortality. So, when this corruptible*

has put on incorruption, and this mortal has put on
immortality, then shall be brought to pass the saying that
is written: "Death is swallowed up in victory." "O Death,
where is your sting? O Hades, where is your victory?"

Antares is the 16th-brightest star in the sky and 16 is the biblical number that represents the love of God. The heart of the King is greater than the heart of death, and it is the love of God that will soundly defeat and bring an end to death for all of us.

Greater love has no one than this, than
to lay down one's life for his friends.

JOHN 15:13

She is not afraid of the snow for her household,
For all her household are clothed with scarlet.

PROVERBS 31:21

Just like the wise woman in Proverbs 31 who has clothed her generations in prayer and trained them up in the ways of the Lord, anyone who calls on the name of Jesus is covered by His blood—His wounds overcome fear and death itself. That is love.

Sixteen and the Love of God

Like I mentioned above, 16 is the number God uses to point to His great love for us. While there are 16 attributes of love in 1 Corinthians 13, there are also 16 "baptisms" throughout the Word and 16 commands given to the nation of Israel. Acts 15:25 tells that the 16th time Paul's name is mentioned in scripture, he is called "Beloved."

As you grow in the love of God, you grow in your understanding of the 16 faces of His Jehovah titles:

- Jehovah Elohim—The Lord Eternal or Creator
- Jehovah Adonai—The Lord our Master
- Jehovah Jireh—The Lord our Provider
- Jehovah Nissi—The Lord our Banner
- Jehovah Rapha—The Lord our Healer
- Jehovah Shalom—The Lord our Peace
- Jehovah Tsidkenu—The Lord our Righteousness
- Jehovah M'kaddish—The Lord our Sanctifier
- Jehovah Sabbath—The Lord of Hosts
- Jehovah Shaman—The Lord is Present
- Jehovah Elyon—The Lord Most High
- Jehovah Rohi—The Lord my Shepherd
- Jehovah Hoseenu—The Lord our Maker
- Jehovah Eloheenu—The Lord our God
- Jehovah Eloheeka—The Lord your God
- Jehovah Elohay—The Lord my God

Scorpio is the sign that promises death will be overcome through a war won by the love of Almighty God.

Star Party

- Scorpio is the southernmost constellation in the Zodiac.
- From the northern hemisphere, it is highest in the evening on the hot summer nights of July and August.

- It contains a number of notable stars and deep sky objects, including the bright stars Antares and Shaula, the Butterfly Cluster (Messier 6), the Ptolemy Cluster (Messier 7), Cat's Paw Nebula (NGC 6334), the Butterfly Nebula (NGC 6302), and the War and Peace Nebula (NGC 6357). Do a Google search and look these up.

- Antares pumps out more than 60,000 times the energy of our Sun!

- Antares is thought to be 604 light-years away.

- Antares is a red super giant that is so huge it boggles the mind! If it were in the same spot as our Sun, the Earth's orbit would still be under its surface, and it would nearly touch the orbit of Jupiter!

- There is a big argument over which is bigger, Betelgeuse or Antares. The reason is because they are both variable stars that fluctuate in size. In science, the two stars are comparable in so many ways, and again, we have the battle between the Coming Branch (Betelgeuse) and the heart of darkness (Antares). To get a better understanding, see my chapter on Orion and on things that blow my mind.

The Heavens Declare the Glory of God

–SIGN 4–

SAGITTARIUS THE ARCHER

The Prophetic Promise: Our Redeemer Will Win the Ultimate War upon Our Behalf.

When the perishable puts on the imperishable, and the mortal puts on immortality, then shall come to pass the saying that is written: "Death is swallowed up in victory." "O death, where is your victory? O death, where is your sting?" The sting of death is sin, and the power of sin is the law.But thanks be to God, who gives us the victory through our Lord Jesus Christ.

1 CORINTHIANS 15:54-57 ESV

Here, the Messiah is prophesied as an archer and a man of great warfare who is not afraid to deal with the enormous problem of the scorpion (death). He is seen as a man of war on a horse, and His arrow is pointed directly at the heart of the scorpion. He is strong, full of grace, and dual natured. This is the King of Kings as seen in Revelation coming to conquer death.

And He who sat there was like a jasper and a sardius stone in appearance; and there was a rainbow around the throne, in appearance like an emerald.

REVELATION 4:3

A bow and arrow prophetically represent deliverance.

And he said, "Open the east window"; and he opened it. Then Elisha said, "Shoot"; and he shot.

*And he said, "The arrow of the Lord's deliverance
and the arrow of deliverance from Syria."*

2 KINGS 13:17

Looking Up: Behold! The Archer of Heaven!

A strong bow represents covenant, and in part four of our dramatic promise of redemption, we see He is one who will keep His promises.

*I set My **rainbow** in the cloud, and it shall be for
the sign of the covenant between Me and the earth.*

GENESIS 9:13

*And I looked, and behold, a white horse. He who
sat on it had a bow; and a crown was given to
him, and he went out conquering and to conquer.*

REVELATION 6:2

Dual-Natured and Riding a Horse of War

He is portrayed by the Greeks to be a centaur—half man and half horse. They almost have the picture, but not quite. He is actually a warrior who mysteriously has two distinct natures— He is both God and human being. Jesus Christ is the God-man and in this sign, He is riding on a war horse.

Verses telling us Jesus is fully God:

Isaiah 9:6; Matthew 11:27; 16:16; Mark 2:5-7; Luke 5:20-22; 9:20; John 1:1; 1:14; 2:19, 21; 3:13, 31; 5:18; 6:38; 8:58; 9: 38; 10:17; 10:30; 13:3; 14:9; 14:23; 16:15; 16:28; 17:8; 17:21-23; 20:28; Romans 9:5; 1 Corinthians 10:3-4; 15:47; 18:4-6; 2 Corinthians 8:9; Philippians 2:5-11; Colossians 1:15-17, 19; 2:9;

1 Timothy 1:17; 2:5; Titus 2:13; Hebrews 1:2-3, 8-11; 2:7, 9, 14, 16; 13:8; 1 John 5:20; Revelation 1:8, 17; 2:8; 3:14.

Verses telling us Jesus is fully human:

Matthew 1:1, 18-25; 4:2; 26:38; Luke 1:26-38; 9:58; 22:44; John 1:14; 11:33-35; 19:28, 34; Romans 9:5; 1 Corinthians 15:3; Galatians 4:4; Philippians 2:5-11; 1 Timothy 2:5; 3:16; Hebrews 2:14-15, 17-18; 4:15; 10:5; 1 Peter 2:24; 1 John 4:2; 2 John 7.

Names of the Brightest Stars

Al Naim, "the gracious one":

> And the God of peace will crush Satan under your feet shortly. The grace of our Lord Jesus Christ be with you. Amen.

ROMANS 16:20

Al Shaula, "the dart":

> And Moses stretched out his rod toward heaven; and the Lord sent thunder and hail, and fire darted to the ground. And the Lord rained hail on the land of Egypt.

EXODUS 9:23

Al Warida, "who comes forth":

> And I looked, and behold, a white horse. He who sat on it had a bow; and a crown was given to him, and he went out conquering and to conquer.

REVELATION 6:2

Ruchba or Rami, "the riding of the bowman":

*Now I saw heaven opened, and behold, a white horse.
And He who sat on him was called Faithful and
True, and in righteousness He judges and makes war.*

REVELATION 19:11

*And the armies in heaven, clothed in fine linen,
white and clean, followed Him on white horses.*

REVELATION 19:14

Nun-ki, "The Prince of the Earth":

By me princes rule, and nobles, all the judges of the earth.

PROVERBS 8:16

*But God shall shoot at them with an arrow; Suddenly they
shall be wounded. So He will make them stumble over their
own tongue; All who see them shall flee away. All men shall
fear, And shall declare the work of God; For they shall wisely
consider His doing. The righteous shall be glad in the Lord,
and trust in Him. And all the upright in heart shall glory.*

PSALM 64:7-10

Star Party

- If you're outside on an August or September evening, you can glimpse the constellation Sagittarius the Archer. From our northern latitudes, it never climbs high in the sky. Yet Sagittarius points to one of the most wondrous places we can imagine; the center of our own Milky Way Galaxy! It's actually fairly easy to spot, because its brightest stars form a distinctive shape of a teapot. Here's another way to find Sagittarius: if you're familiar with the Summer Triangle, draw an imaginary line from the star Deneb, through the star Altair to locate Sagittarius near the horizon. Boom!

- The very center of our galaxy was discovered to be near the tip of the arrow of Sagittarius. Can you imagine? There was an arrow pointing to it the whole time!

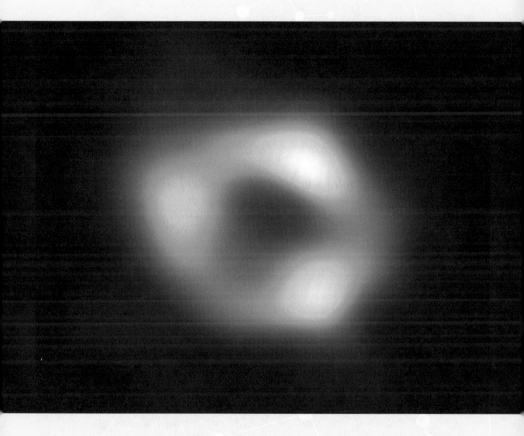

This photograph, taken by NASA using a very powerful lunar camera aimed at the recently discovered center of the Milky Way Galaxy, is an amazing prophetic word that supports what we've uncovered about Sagittarius. The tip of his arrow is literally a ring of fire around what scientists believe to be a black hole. It's a Trinity set in a ring of covenant that shouts, "Death will not part us forever! I promise I am coming and I will rescue you by destroying the enemy–death itself."

> *"For I," says the Lord, "will be a wall of fire all*
> *around her, and I will be the glory in her midst."*

ZECHARIAH 2:5

And the black hole at the very center? Not only does this photograph prophesy that darkness is overcome, it is a picture of death being swallowed up by life. It has no place in eternity.

> *So when this corruptible has put on incorruption, and this*
> *mortal has put on immortality, then shall be brought to pass*
> *the saying that is written: "Death is swallowed up in victory."*

1 CORINTHIANS 15:54

> *All the host of heaven shall be dissolved, And*
> *the heavens shall be rolled up like a scroll....*

ISAIAH 34:4

> *Then the sky receded as a scroll when it is rolled up, and*
> *every mountain and island was moved out of its place.*

REVELATION 6:14

> *Then I saw a great white throne and Him who*
> *sat on it, from whose face the earth and the heaven*
> *fled away. And there was found no place for them.*

REVELATION 20:11

- The Sagittarius Star Cloud, about 30,000 light-years in distance, seems to be the nucleus. That means it would take us 30,000 years traveling at the speed of light to reach the center of our galaxy. With the Sun, and all the outer stars of our solar system turning at the rate of 155 miles per second, it requires about 200 million of our earthly years for our galaxy to make one complete revolution, called a "cosmic year." The star cloud's outer edge is about 20,000 light-years in the opposite direction. The Milky Way is bigger than we can imagine, yet it is only one of billions.

- The brightest star in Sagittarius is the 36th-brightest star in the sky, 125 light-years away and 375 times brighter than the Sun.

The Heavens Declare the Glory of God.

-SIGN 5-

CAPRICORN THE SEA GOAT

The Prophetic Promise: Those Redeemed Would Become One Body with the Messiah.

*For even the Son of Man did not come to be served,
but to serve, and to give His life a ransom for many.*

MARK 10:45

There is no such thing as a sea goat, just like there is no such thing as a centaur. In the last sign, Sagittarius, we were presented with the mystery of the dual nature of Jesus as both God and man at the same time. Now, in this prophetic sign of the heavens, we are presented with the mystery of the Redeemer and the redeemed as one body. In this picture in the heavens, the Goat is pictured as bowing its head as though he is dying, and its right leg is folded underneath the body, as if he is laying down his life. The tail of the fish is not like that, but alive and splashing around. When you understand that the goat is before and the fish is after, then you understand what the prophetic picture is all about.

The Goat Is the Sacrifice.

(LEVITICUS 10:16,17; 16:22)

The Fish Are Those The Sacrifice Was Paid For.

(MATTHEW 4:19; JEREMIAH 16:16)

The Sea Goat and Fish Are the Two Becoming One Body–Both Fully Resurrected and Redeemed.

This sign is fulfilled in John 17:20-23:

> *I do not pray for these alone, but also for those who will believe in Me through their word; that they all may be one, as You, Father, are in Me, and I in You; that they also may be one in Us, that the world may believe that You sent Me. And the glory which You gave Me I have given them, that they may be one just as We are one: I in them, and You in Me; that they may be made perfect in one, and that the world may know that You have sent Me, and have loved them as You have loved Me.*

So out of His death (the goat), we would come to life (the fish), and be joined to Him as one (the sea goat).

Looking Up

Capricorn is the second dimmest of all the constellations, behind only Cancer. Prophetically, this speaks of mystery and the necessity of searching out the matter in order to understand what is being said here.

> *It is the glory of God to conceal a matter, but*
> *the glory of kings is to search out a matter.*

PROVERBS 25:2

Traditionally, there are 51 stars in Capricorn. Five are what Bullinger calls "remarkable stars." The brightest star is Deneb Algedi, "the sacrifice is coming." This is the promise of the Messiah/ Redeemer.

Names of other stars in Capricorn are:

- Dabih: "the sacrifice"
- Al Dabik and Al Dehabeh mean the same thing as Dibiah Nishira: "the bringer of good tidings" (Luke 4:18)
- Ma'asad: "the one being slain"
- Sa'ad al Naschira: "the testimony of the separated" (2 Corinthians 6:17)

Star Party

- To find arrowhead-shaped Capricorn in the sky, look for the Summer Triangle and make a line from Vega through Altair to the lower southern sky. Remember, it is faint but you know you have found it when you spot the triangle shape.
- In the northern hemisphere, Capricorn can be seen from July to November.
- The area of the night sky in which Capricorn is located is known as the "Sea."
- The "Sea" is mostly inhabited by other "watery" constellations such as Pisces and Aquarius.
- Also known as Delta Capricorni, Deneb Algedi is a binary star system around 40 light-years from Earth. It is the primary star in the system, and is a white giant with a mass and radius around twice that of our Sun.
- The number 40 in scripture is used often to signify a time of trial or testing–usually pointing to when that trial is over. As Deneb Algedi means "the sacrifice is

coming," that lets us know our time of trial is coming to an end. The Redeemer is on the way.

- Nashira, the faint star just next to the brightest star, also known as Gamma Capricorni, is a white giant star around 140 light-years from Earth.

The number 140 in the Strong's Greek Concordance is the word "hairetizó: to choose; chosen." It is found in one place only in the Bible and speaks of the Only one who can save us. I believe it also declares He will redeem the stolen story in the stars as wrongly believed by the Gentile nations who were led astray.

Behold! My Servant whom I have chosen, My Beloved in whom My soul is well pleased! I will put My Spirit upon Him, And He will declare justice to the Gentiles.

MATTHEW 12:18

The Heavens Declare the Glory of God.

–SIGN 6–

AQUARIUS THE WATER BEARER

The Prophetic Promise: The Holy Spirit Would Be Poured Out upon All Those Redeemed.

And it shall come to pass in the last days, says God,
That I will pour out of My Spirit on all flesh;
Your sons and your daughters shall prophesy,
Your young men shall see visions,
Your old men shall dream dreams.

Acts 2:17

Now that we've seen that a redeemed people come from the sacrifice, a new picture in the heavens rises up proclaiming that God will pour out His Spirit upon them. This is Aquarius the Water Bearer.

Looking Up

This is a picture of a man pouring water out upon little fish. In some of the oldest pictures, He is seen as pouring out water with fish in the water, but all of the pictures agree as to what this is representing. This is the picture of God's goodness. This is how God blesses His people by pouring out His Holy Spirit and resurrection power upon those who are His. Isaiah 44:1-3 says:

Yet hear now, O Jacob My servant,
And Israel whom I have chosen.
Thus says the Lord who made you

And formed you from the womb, who will help you:
"Fear not, O Jacob My servant;
And you, Jeshurun, whom I have chosen.
For I will pour water on him who is thirsty,
And floods on the dry ground;
I will pour My Spirit on your descendants,
And My blessing on your offspring."

Before that was written in the Bible, it was written in the heavens because the Author is the same.

Aquarius is pouring out His blessing. He is pouring out something He couldn't until He had dealt with the enemy, death, at Sagittarius. He is giving out resurrection power and life!

This Is Exactly What Jesus Christ Did for Us after His Resurrection!

For you did not receive the spirit of slavery to
fall back into fear, but you have received the
Spirit of adoption as sons, by whom we cry,
"Abba! Father!"

ROMANS 8:15 ESV

But if the Spirit of Him who raised Jesus from the
dead dwells in you, He who raised Christ Jesus
from the dead will also give life to your mortal
bodies through His Spirit who dwells in you.

ROMANS 8:11

What agreement has the temple of God with idols? For
we are the temple of the living God; as God said, "I will

make my dwelling among them and walk among them,
and I will be their God, and they shall be my people."

2 CORINTHIANS 6:16

Traditionally, there are 108 stars in this sign. The brightest star—located in the right shoulder—is called Sa'ad al Melik, which means "the record of the pouring forth." The star of the left shoulder is called Saad al Sund, meaning "who goes and returns." Now we first see the revelation that Christ will come twice. He is pouring out His Spirit during the time between His first coming and His second coming. Amazing!

The name of the next brightest star says the same thing. The bright star in the lower part of his right leg is the Hebrew name Scheat, which means "who is going away and returning again." Boom! There is it again! It is literally written in the heavens that after the resurrection, He would leave with the promise of returning. He will not leave us alone, but He will pour His Spirit out upon us.

How lovely are your tents, O Jacob!
Your dwellings, O Israel!
Like valleys that stretch out,
Like gardens by the riverside,
Like aloes planted by the Lord,
Like cedars beside the waters.
He shall pour water from his buckets,
And his seed shall be in many waters.
"His king shall be higher than Agag,
And his kingdom shall be exalted."

NUMBERS 24:5-7

Star Party

- The passing of the autumn equinox means the days are beginning to shorten and weather is becoming colder for people in the northern hemisphere. Aquarius shows us that the season has changed.

- The original Aqua-Man is best seen in the evening sky during the fall. You'll see Aquarius highest in the sky in early October around 10 -11 p.m. local time, or you can spot him in early November around 8 p.m.

- Aquarius is located in a region of the sky sometimes called the "Sea" because so many of the signs have something to do with water.

- Aquarius has almost universally been associated with water and the rainy seasons.

- Aquarius is home to four meteor showers which occur throughout the year. The greatest is called the Delta Aquarid Meteor shower (July 14-August 18), which can produce around 20 meteors per hour at its peak.

- The second-brightest star in Aquarius is the yellow super giant Sadalsuud, which is 537 light-years distant. The number 537 in the Strong's Greek Concordance is the word "Hapas: all the whole." Through these verse where "hapas" appears, it speaks prophetically about this sign and testifies to the one the sign represents.

...and did not know until the flood came and took them all away, so also will the coming of the Son of Man be.

MATTHEW 24:39

When all the people were baptized, it came to pass that Jesus also was baptized; and while He prayed, the heaven was opened.

LUKE 3:21

The Heavens Declare the Glory of God.

–SIGN 7–

PISCES THE FISH

The Prophetic Promise: The Messiah Would Have a Blessed People and They Would Be Greatly Multiplied.

Blessing I will bless you, and multiplying I will multiply your descendants as the stars of the heavens and as the sand which is on the seashore; and your descendants shall possess the gate of their enemies.

GENESIS 22:17

Pisces represents the seed of Abraham and those in covenant with God. There are two different kinds of covenants: natural and supernatural.

The sign of Pisces is located in the part of the sky known as the Sea. This part of the rotating drama represents the work of Jesus in the world (the sea) between His first and second coming.

Looking Up

Pisces is a symbol of two fishes tied together at the tail by a band. One of them is pointed vertically toward the North Star. The other is represented as horizontal and is swimming in the flow of the ecliptic, or the "path of the Sun." Take note: anytime you see the Sun prophetically in the Bible, you are being instructed to look at natural events. A good example of this is found in the book of Revelation.

Now a great sign appeared in heaven: a woman
clothed with the sun, with the moon under her
feet, and on her head a garland of twelve stars.

REVELATION 12:1

Here you have three different realms of things going on:

1. The woman clothed in the Sun is natural Israel.

2. The moon under her feet is the Church, which is no longer center stage during the tribulation, but has a profound impact on natural Israel as she is beginning to stand with the Church.

3. Then there are the stars of Heaven, which represent the supernatural sons and daughters of God (people of faith) who are now being seen as a crown in natural Israel.

This is the convergence of so many prayers, hopes, dreams and intentions of God Almighty Himself! At this point in the tribulation, the great dragon is there to devour the offspring of this woman.

The point is, one of these fish represents God's natural nation (Israel) and the other represents God's supernatural nation (Christianity). This was the promise God gave to Abraham: that his offspring would be as the sands of the sea (natural) and as the stars of Heaven (supernatural). In other words, those who are born Jews and those who are born again "inwardly" as Jews. Awesome!

...but he is a Jew who is one inwardly; and
circumcision is that of the heart, in the Spirit, not in
the letter; whose praise is not from men but from God.

ROMANS 2:29

Fishing on the High Side of the Boat

Do you see it? These two fish look like a cross, one vertical and one horizontal! This is the sign that says Heaven will invade earth through His people. There they are, fully redeemed by the Redeemer Himself on that ancient Roman instrument of death and shame. God's people are seen as righteous, blessed and greatly multiplied.

> *Blessed is the nation whose God is the Lord, the people He has chosen as His own inheritance.*

> PSALM 33:12

This is the sign that represents the abundant life Jesus is giving to His people.

> *...I have come that they may have life, and that they may have it more abundantly.*

> JOHN 10:10

The Egyptian name for Pisces is Pi-cot Orion, or Pisces Hori, which means "the fishes of Him that is coming." So there it is again. The Master has gone to prepare a place for His people. These are His people and He will come back again.

The Hebrew name for Pisces is Dagim. If you will remember, the Philistines worshipped a fish god called Dagon. They also had a cult which worshipped Pisces. Dagim means "the Fishes," and it has to do with a word that means "multitudes."

> *Let them grow into a multitude in the midst of the earth.*

> GENESIS 48:16

The next day a great multitude that had come to the feast,
when they heard that Jesus was coming to Jerusalem.

JOHN 12:12

Now it happened in Iconium that they went together
to the synagogue of the Jews, and so spoke that a great
multitude both of the Jews and of the Greeks believed.

ACTS 14:1

And some of them were persuaded; and a great
multitude of the devout Greeks, and not a few
of the leading women, joined Paul and Silas.

ACTS 17:4

After these things I looked, and behold, a great multitude
which no one could number, of all nations, tribes, peoples,
and tongues, standing before the throne and before the Lamb,
clothed with white robes, with palm branches in their hands.

REVELATION 7:9

After these things I heard a loud voice of a great
multitude in heaven, saying, "Alleluia! Salvation and
glory and honor and power belong to the Lord our God!"

REVELATION 19:1

So Pisces represents the people of God, both natural and
supernatural. It represents the multiplied blessing of residents
of Heaven living on the Earth waiting upon the return of Jesus
Christ. It also represents the Gospel of Jesus Christ and the
presence of the Lord being carried to the entire reaches of the
planet Earth through His blessed people.

Star Party

- As seen from across the globe, Pisces reaches its high point for the night at about 10 p.m. local standard time in early November, and at about 8 p.m. in early December.

- Pisces is a large but faint constellation containing no bright stars.

- The constellation is only fully visible in areas away from light pollution.

- If you can find the great square of Pegasus, you can find our faint Pisces fishes because the beautiful V shape is sliding toward the center of the band.

- The brightest star in Pisces is discovered to be 316 light-years away. It is called Kullat Nunu, which means "the chord of the fish." It is classified as a bright giant star with a luminosity 316 times that of the Sun. It is located 294 light-years from Earth.

- Remember, Pieces represents saved people with a message of hope for the rest of the world. Guess what John 3:16 says? *"For God so loved the world that He gave His only begotten Son, that whoever believes in Him should not perish but have everlasting life."* This is the message of the multiplied fish in the Earth.

Names of other stars in Pisces are:

- Fum al Samakah: "mouth of the fish," located 492 light-years away.

- Linteum: "the cord," located 305 light-years away. It is a class K5III star with an apparent 44.4 magnitude. In the Strong's Greek Concordance, 444 is the word "anthrópos: a man, human, mankind." You will never believe what verse contains the word "anthropos": Matthew 4:19 which says, *"Then He said to them, "Follow Me, and I will make you fishers of men."* If that's not enough, check out Isaiah 44:4: *"They will spring up among the grass, Like willows by the watercourses."*

- Kaht: also "cord," located 190 light-years away. It is a class K0III star with an apparent magnitude of 4.27.

- Revati: "rich or blessed," located 148 light-years away. It is a class A7IV star with an apparent magnitude of 5.21. What does John 5:21 say? *"For as the Father raises the dead and gives life to them, even so the Son gives life to whom He will."*

- Torcular: "thread or tether," located 258 light-years away. It is a class K0III star with an apparent 4.2 magnitude.

- Vernalis: referring to the vernal equinox, it is located 106 light-years away. It is a class F4IV star with an apparent magnitude of 4.03. The number 106 in the Strong's Greek Concordance is the word "azumos: unleavened." It's all about how the sacrifice of Jesus and the outpouring of the Holy Spirit made us new.

Therefore purge out the old leaven, that you may be a new lump, since you truly are unleavened. For indeed Christ, our Passover, was sacrificed for us.

1 Corinthians 5:7

The Heavens Declare the Glory of God.

–SIGN 8–

ARIES THE RAM

The Prophetic Promise: The One Who Was Slain for Our Atonement Would Be Given All Power and Authority to Make All Things New.

*And Jesus came and spake unto them, saying,
All power is given unto me in heaven and earth.*

MATTHEW 28:18 KJV

I have already stated that the story begins at Virgo (Genesis 3) and ends with Leo (Revelation 21). This is in accordance to the sequence of Revelation, and matches the Sphinx (head of a woman, body of a lion). This is totally different from how the rest of the world views the Zodiac. Astrologers begin at Aries and end with Pisces because Spring starts in Aries. The bottom line here is, they have the facts, but they do not have the revelation. Why? The plan of redemption is hidden from idol worshippers, or idolaters.

*Those who make an image, all of them are useless, and their
precious things shall not profit; they are their own witnesses;
they neither see nor know, that they may be ashamed.*

ISAIAH 44:9

*They do not know nor understand; for he has
shut their eyes, so that they cannot see, and
their hearts, so that they cannot understand.*

ISAIAH 44:18

New Beginnings

The constellation Aries is all about the power of atonement and that Jesus makes all things brand-new. Idolaters throughout the centuries have seen something like this, but couldn't quite figure it out. Bullinger writes that according to Herodotus, a Greek historian who lived at the same time as Socrates, the ancient Egyptians would have a new year party at the entrance of the Sun into Aries. They would slay a ram and place branches over the doors of their homes.

It wasn't much of a leap for God to tell His people that they were to slay a lamb at the same exact time, and place the blood on the doorposts of their homes for the very first Passover. This was the emancipation from slavery for God's people, and it starts with the blood of the lamb (Exodus 11).

Years later, the Sun entered Aries on the 14th of the Jewish month Nisan. Jesus Christ, the Lamb who takes away the sins of the world, was slain on Passover day in Jerusalem. This was the emancipation from slavery for all who would believe. It was the beginning of something brand-new, and that's what Aries is about. The POWER of Redemption and the newness of life.

> *Then He who sat on the throne said,*
> *"Behold, I make all things new."*
> *And He said to me,*
> *"Write, for these words are true and faithful."*
>
> REVELATION 21:5

Looking Up

Aries is pictured as a ram, or lamb, strong and full of life. He looks a lot different than the picture of Capricorn, where he is falling down and dying. Aries is all about this lamb ruling and reigning. It is the sign that represents the Kingdom of God coming into the Earth and His people overcoming victoriously.

And they overcame him by the blood of the
Lamb and by the word of their testimony....

REVELATION 12:11

Your kingdom come. Your will be
done on earth as it is in heaven.

MATTHEW 6:10

In the Denderah Zodiac, it's called Tametouris Ammon, which means "the ruling or reigning or dominion and power or government of Ammon." The lamb's head is pictured without horns, and is crowned with a circle, the mark of divinity similar to what we call a halo. In Hebrew, it is called Taleh, "the lamb." The ancient Akkadian name was Bara-ziggar. *Bar* means "sacrifice" and *ziggar* means "right making." So they called the sign "the sacrifice of righteousness."

Behold the Lamb of God who
takes away the sin of the world!

JOHN 1:29

There are 66 stars in this sign, and there are 66 books in the Bible. The Bible and this constellation agree: the Lamb laid down His life as a sacrifice so that we should be righteous. He now has the power to make all things new. They both testify to Jesus Christ.

You search the Scriptures, for in them, you think you
have eternal life; and these are they which testify of Me.

JOHN 5:39

> *...saying with a loud voice: "Worthy is the Lamb who*
> *was slain to receive power and riches and wisdom,*
> *and strength and honor and glory and blessing!"*

REVELATION 5:12

If that doesn't blow your mind, then let's add this: Aries' brightest star is Alpha Arietis, which was first known as El Nath. It is an orange giant that is exactly 66 light-years from Earth! Sixty-six books in the Bible, 66 stars in the constellation and the brightest star is 66 light-years away! Sixty-six is a number associated with the witness and the testimony of Jesus Christ to all flesh. That same bright star is also called Hamal, which is the Arabic word for "lamb" or "head of the ram."

The Isaiah Prophecy

You'll love this! The brightest star in Aries is named El Nath, or El Natik, which means "wounded, slain." The next brightest star is called Al Sheratan, "the bruised, the wounded." The third-brightest is called Mesarim (Hebrew), "the bound." Doesn't that remind you of another biblical prophecy?

> *But He was wounded for our transgressions* [El
> Natik], *He was bruised for our iniquities* [Al
> Sheratan]; *The chastisement for our peace was upon*
> *Him* [Mesarim], *and by His stripes we are healed.*

ISAIAH 53:5

Before that prophecy was in the Bible, it was in the heavens and in the constellation Aries. The crowned King was as a Lamb once sacrificed, because the Author of the Bible and the heavens is the same.

Star Party

- Aries is located in the northern hemisphere between Pisces to its west and Taurus to its east.

- Aries is best viewed in December at 9 p.m. local time.

- The brightest star, Alpha Arietis, has a planet circling it which is several times bigger than Jupiter.

- The second-brightest star, Sheratan, is a blue-white star located 59 light-years away from Earth.

- Other notable stars in the Aries constellation are: Lambda Arietis, a binary star with a yellow-white dwarf for a primary; Pi Arietis, a star system 603 light-years distant, with a blue-white dwarf for a primary; Arietis or Bharani, a variable star 160 light-years away from Earth.

- Look up Teegarden's Star on Google. It's an interesting read on a tiny star in Aries, and one of the closest to our Sun. It is only 12 light-years away and is only as big as Jupiter. It is thought to have a system of small planets like Jupiter's moons.

The Heavens Declare the Glory of God.

–SIGN 9–

TAURUS THE BULL

The Prophetic Promise: The Messiah Will Come Back with His People to Judge, to Rule and to Reign.

Let not your heart be troubled; you believe in God, believe also in Me. In My Father's house are many mansions; if it were not so, I would have told you. I go to prepare a place for you. And if I go and prepare a place for you, I will come again and receive you to Myself; that where I am, there you may be also.

JOHN 14:1-3

Everything changes again at this constellation. We are now leaving the part of the heavens called "the sea," and now something very different is portrayed. The story of redemption as seen in the heavens is divided into three different parts, or acts, as stated in Chapter One "How It All Works." This is stage three and the grand finale. Taurus the Bull tells us that Jesus is coming back and nothing can stop Him!

Looking Up

Taurus is a bull seen rushing forward in progression with an unstoppable momentum. He is seen as having fierce wrath and His horns are set against the enemy.

The Egyptians called this sign "Mighty Isis," who was a demonic spirit who has now attached itself to Muslims throughout the world. However, *isis* is a word that means "saves or delivers," and this is actually Jesus coming back to save Israel! I bet the Muslims of Isis today would choke on that revelation!

The more common Hebrew name for Taurus was Shur, which is from a root which means both "coming" and "ruling." It is exactly what our Messiah Redeemer is coming back to do—take the horn to His enemies and rule and reign.

The stars in Taurus are very different from the other constellations because within the constellation of stars are two star clusters. Let's look at this.

The brightest star, located in the bull's-eye, is a star called Al Debaran, and means the "leader or governor." Here, Jesus is leading His Church back to Earth in a victorious battle.

> *The LORD thunders at the head of his army;*
> *his forces are beyond number,*
> *and mighty is the army that obeys his command.*
> *The day of the LORD is great; it is dreadful.*
> *Who can endure it?*

JOEL 2:11 NIV

> *And the armies which were in heaven followed him*
> *upon white horses, clothed in fine linen, white and clean.*

REVELATION 19:14 KJV

The star located at the tip of the left horn has an Arabic name, El Nath, meaning "wounded or slain." Just like we have seen in Aries, this is the Lamb who was slain from the foundation of the world coming back to lead His armies (Revelation 13:8). However, now He is seen as all-powerful and unstoppable.

The Magnificent Seven

In the neck of Taurus the Bull, is the cluster of stars known as the Pleiades, which means "the congregation of the judge." It is the same as Ursa Major and Ursa Minor. It represents the seven stars, or the seven churches in the book of Revelation. They are always seen as the "seven sisters" and the "daughters of the King." When you overlay a map of the Pleiades with the location of the seven churches of Revelation 2 and 3, you'll be amazed. Check this out:

Within the face of Taurus the Bull, is the star cluster known as the Hyades, which means "the congregation." This is almost exactly the same picture as the Pleiades in the neck. This place on the neck represents that we are kept in His strong will toward us. The place on the face represents how we personally know Him. The Pleiades are the "Daughters of the King," protected, led and loved. The Hyades are the "Harem of the King," protected, led, and loved. The Church will be caught up to live forever with the Lord (1 Thessalonians 4:17). Then we will return with Him, safe from all judgment, born of Him, and as His bride. This is what Taurus told us in the night sky before the word was written in the Bible.

For your Maker is your husband,
the LORD of hosts is his name;
and the Holy One of Israel is your Redeemer,
the God of the whole earth he is called.

Isaiah 54:5 ESV

The Pleiades have many names. Some of them are:

- Al Clone, which means "the center," has given the idea to some astronomers that it is the center of the whole universe. I don't know about that, but I know His love is centered on us.

- Palilicium (Hebrew), "belonging to the judge"

- Wasat (Arabic), "center or foundation"

- Al Thuraiya (Arabic), "the abundance"

This is the hope of the story of redemption: that Jesus Christ is coming again to destroy the enemies of God's people, and when He does, we will be riding with Him free from His judgment.

Star Party

- Taurus the Bull passes through the sky from November to March, but is most visible in January.

- Taurus is located between the constellations Aries and Gemini.

- Babylonian astronomers called the constellation the "Heavenly Bull." Ancient Egyptians believed it represented a sacred bull, one associated with the renewal of nature in spring.

- The brightest star in the constellation is Aldebaran, which means "the leader or follow the leader." Aldebaran is an orange-red giant, an irregular variable star, about 66 light-years away. Another testimony of the 66 books of the Bible and the one they testify of—King Jesus!

- The second-brightest star lies near the border with the constellation Auriga. It is sometimes called El Nath or Alnath, meaning "the bull's horns." El Nath is a B-class star evolving into a giant. It lies about 131 light-years from Earth. Though it is short, Psalm 131 is titled "Simple Trust in the Lord" and is a song of Ascents, the staircase, or "going up." It is a prophetic picture of grabbing the bull by the horns on the brazen altar. These horns are symbolic of God's great mercy and breakthrough power to rescue us. See below.

- Alcyone is the brightest of the Pleiades and the third-brightest star in Taurus. It is a multiple-star system with a blue-white giant for a primary component. Alcyone is 440 light-years distant. In the Strong's Greek Concordance, 440 is associated with the word "anthrax: coal, charcoal" and is found in Romans 12:20. Look it up! Jesus truly did heap coals on the enemy's head on our behalf.

- Epsilon Tauri, also known as Ain, which means "eye," and Oculus Borealis, meaning "northern eye," is an orange giant, 147 light-years distant. It belongs to the Hyades cluster, the nearest open cluster to our solar system, and is only 151 light-years away.

- The Hyades cluster contains 300-400 stars. The brightest ones form the shape of the letter V, which appears along the same line of sight as Aldebaran, a star that is not a member of the cluster.

It is amazing to me that Taurus represents the hope of Israel, because in Psalm 131 it says,

> *O Israel, hope in the Lord*
> *From this time forth and forever.*

PSALM 131:3

The Heavens Declare the Glory of God.

–SIGN 10–

GEMINI THE TWINS

The Prophetic Promise: Those Redeemed Will Be Righteous as the One Who Redeemed Them.

For now we see in a mirror, dimly, but then face to face. Now I know in part, but then I shall know just as I also am known.

1 CORINTHIANS 13:12

Now we come to Gemini the Twins. These twins have been the stars pagans prayed to for the purpose of navigation. In Acts chapter 28, Castor and Pollux was the name of the boat that sank. Paul mentions it because the pagan gods couldn't keep it afloat. It was also the sign that the Romans and Greeks swore by. "By Gemini" was something that people swore on in Roman culture, and was probably what Jesus was talking about when He said,

But I say to you, do not swear at all: neither by heaven, for it is God's throne.

MATTHEW 5:34

There was some kind of a hope presented in this constellation and the ancients who didn't know God, tried to imagine what that could be. This influence through the ages must have been what the Disney writers were referring to when they had Jiminy (or Gemini) Cricket sing, "When you wish upon a star." Gemini's theme of hope has always had influence on cultures. And just like Pinocchio turning into a real boy, those redeemed would be born again into the likeness of their Creator, God Himself. This is what Gemini is all about.

Looking Up

The Twins in the heavens are seen as having not been born at the same time, but united by covenant—just alike in peace and in harmony. There is no scene of war here, but a picture of perfect brotherhood.

Gemini's name in the Denderah Zodiac is Claustrum Hor, which means "the place of Him who comes." When Jesus comes, we have an amazing place with Him. In Hebrew, this is called Thaumim, which means "united." We first saw a glimpse of this in Capricorn where the body of the fish (the Church) is united with the body of the Goat (Jesus slain), but they are two different bodies.

Now I am no longer in the world, but these are
in the world, and I come to You. Holy Father,
keep through Your name those whom You have
given Me, that they may be one as We are.

JOHN 17:11

And the glory which You gave Me I have given
them, that they may be one just as We are one....

JOHN 17:22

In Gemini, the bodies are different, yet they are twins and you cannot tell the difference between the two. This is the progression of the revelation of our redemption!

This righteousness is given through faith in Jesus Christ to all
who believe. There is no difference between Jew and Gentile....

ROMANS 3:22 NIV

*Beloved, now we are children of God; and it has not yet been
revealed what we shall be, but we know that when He is
revealed, we shall be like Him, for we shall see Him as He is.*

1 JOHN 3:2

One of the twins holds in his right hand a palm branch.
Some pictures show a club, but neither the club nor bow are
in action. These united ones are at rest and in peace after
winning the victory. One is called Propus (Hebrew), meaning
"the branch, spreading." Another is called Al Giauza (Arabic),
which is "the palm branch." Another is named Al Dira (Arabic),
meaning "the seed, or branch."

Names of other stars in Gemini the Twins:

- The brightest star in Gemini is Pollux. Pollux means
  "very sweet."

*We took sweet counsel together,
And walked to the house of God in the throng.*

PSALM 55:14

- The next brightest star is Castor. It means "to excel,
  to shine." This is the hope of the saints!

*Arise, shine;
For your light has come!
And the glory of the Lord is risen
upon you.*

ISAIAH 60:1

- The third-brightest star in Gemini is called Al Hana.
  It means "God's ring" or "God's token of covenant."

But the father said to his servants, "Bring
out the best robe and put it on him, and put
a ring on his hand and sandals on his feet."

LUKE 15:22

- The fourth-brightest star is called Mebsuta. It means "treading under feet." This is the promise that all He is, we will be, and all He has, we will have.

You have made him to have dominion over the works
of Your hands; You have put all things under his feet.

PSALM 8:6

- Names of other Gemini stars show up as a recognized theme. One is called Propus (Hebrew), "the branch, spreading," Al Giauza (Arabic), "the palm branch," Al Dira (Arabic), "the seed, or branch."

The Branch is back and, as promised in Virgo, He is now fulfilled in Gemini and Orion!

Star Party

- You have several months during the year to observe Gemini, which is one of the brighter constellations of the Zodiac. It lights up the early evening sky from January until May, though it'll set in the west two hours earlier with each passing month.

- January and February present a grand time for observing the constellation Gemini because it is high in the east at nightfall, and stays out for most of the night. Gemini climbs highest in the sky around 10 p.m. in early February, and 9 p.m. in late February.

That's local time—the time on your clock—no matter where you live around the globe.

- Gemini stays in view in the evening sky through mid-May. By late May and June, Gemini is found low in the west-northwest corner of the sky at night-fall. Its two brightest stars, Castor and Pollux, fade into the sunset around the June 21 summer solstice, aka the longest day of the year.

- Castor and Pollux represent the heads of the twins. Pollux is an orange-giant star located 35 light-years away, and Castor is a sextuplet star system located 50 light-years from Earth. Yes, Castor is not just one star, it's actually six!

- The star Alhena or Almeisan, has an apparent visual magnitude of 1.9, making it easily visible to the naked eye even in urban regions. Based upon parallax measurements with the Hipparcos satellite, it is 109 light-years from Earth. In the Strong's Greek Concordance, 109 is associated with the word "aér: air." While this word is in the New Testament seven times—the number of completion or end of a timeline—my favorite is this because it portrays us just as we are in Gemini—with Him in the air:

Then we who are alive and remain shall be caught up together with them in the clouds to meet the Lord in the air. And thus we shall always be with the Lord.

1 THESSALONIANS 4:17

- Another noteworthy star is Mekbuda, a super-giant star with a radius about 220,000 times the size of the Sun.

- Look up "The Eskimo Nebula." This mysterious nebula is found in Gemini.

The Heavens Declare the Glory of God.

–SIGN 11–

CANCER THE CRAB

The Prophetic Promise: Once God Has Redeemed His People, He Will Never Let Them Go.

And I give them eternal life, and they shall never perish; neither shall anyone snatch them out of My hand.

JOHN 10:28

Just before we come to the climax of our prophetic story of redemption, God tells us that He is not going to lose what He has worked so hard to gain—us. Our salvation is never in question once we are eternally secured, and our souls will never be on the line again.

Cancer is the sign of the heavens that speaks of eternal security. It didn't start off as a crab. The Greeks perverted it, as did the Babylonians and the Egyptians. The devil hates the idea of our eternal security in Christ. The Jews see crabs as unclean, so the original sign was not a crab. It was the claws. This is the idea of God holding on and never letting go, and it is still in the heavens for us to behold!

Even the word *cancer* is offensive to us today. It is a satanic plot to pervert the idea of eternal security. The disease was first called cancer by the "father of medicine" and Greek physician, Hippocrates (460-370 BC). This is where we get the Hippocratic Oath that physicians take to "do no harm." The picture of cancer as a crab started because the finger-like projections spreading from a cancer were similar to the shape of a crab.

Later, a Roman physician, Galen (130-200 AD), used the term *oncos*, which is Greek for "swelling," to describe tumors. *Oncos* is the root word for "oncology" or "study of cancers" to this day.

Looking Up

The Arabic name for this sign is Al Sartan, which means "who holds or binds," and in Hebrew, it means to "bind together" (Genesis 49:11). The Syriac name, Sartano, means the same thing. The Greek name is Karkinos, which means "holding or encircling," as does the Latin, Cancer, and hence is applied to the crab. The idea is that God has not only redeemed His people, but He is going to keep His people as well. That's what Jesus was talking about when He prayed in the garden.

> *While I was with them in the world, I kept them in Your name. Those whom You gave Me I have kept....*

JOHN 17:12

That's exactly what the Bible says in 1 Peter chapter 1:

> *Blessed be the God and Father of our Lord Jesus Christ, who according to His abundant mercy, has begotten us again to a living hope through the resurrection of Jesus Christ from the dead, to an inheritance incorruptible and undefiled and that does not fade away, reserved in heaven for you, who are kept by the power of God through faith for salvation ready to be revealed in the last time.*

1 PETER 1:3-5

Our salvation is incorruptible! It doesn't fade away. It is kept by His power. This is Cancer the Crab.

The sign contains 83 stars, one of which is of the third magnitude. Seven are of the fourth magnitude, and the remainder of inferior magnitudes. The brightest star, located in the tail, is called Tegmine, which means "holding." The star in the lower large claw is called Acubene, which in Hebrew and Arabic, means "the sheltering" or "hiding place." Another is named Ma'alaph (Arabic), and it means "assembled thousands." We are safe in Jesus.

Star Party

- Cancer lies between Leo the Lion and Gemini the Twins. It is almost impossible to see Cancer as a crab with the naked eye or even binoculars. It looks more like a faint, upside-down Y, and you can spot that. In Hebrew, the letter that represents "Y" is "Yod." Yod looks like an apostrophe and is the smallest (though maybe most important because it is the first letter in both YWHW and Yeshua–God the Father and God the Son) of the entire 22-letter aleph-bet. Suspended in mid-air, Yod is literally known as the "atom" of the consonants and is the form from which all other letters begin and end. Isn't Yeshua the "first and the last; the beginning and the end" of all things including the written word?

- Cancer is the sign of the summer solstice, and represents the Sun at the highest point of summer.

- The brightest star in Cancer, Tegmine, is an orange K-type giant 290 light-years distant from Earth.

- Cancer also has several notable deep sky objects. The Beehive Cluster is a very popular feature among astronomers. Be sure to Google it. Also, it is located right in the center of the constellation. It is an open star cluster, one of the nearest to our solar system. It is most easily observed when Cancer is high in the sky. North of the equator, the best time to see Cancer stretches from February to May.

- Ptolemy described the Beehive Cluster as "the nebulous mass in the breast of Cancer." It was one of the first objects Galileo observed with his telescope in 1609, spotting 40 stars in the cluster. Today, there are about 1,010 high-probability known stars, 68 percent of them red dwarfs.

- Another notable feature in the Cancer constellation is rho-1 Cancri or 55 Cancri, a binary star approximately 40.9 light-years distant from Earth. 55 Cancri consists of a yellow dwarf and a smaller red dwarf, with five planets orbiting the primary star—one terrestrial planet and four gas giants. It is the only planetary system discovered to have five planets and possibly more. 55 Cancri A, classified as a rare "super metal-rich" star, is one of the top 100 target stars for NASA's Terrestrial Planet Finder mission. It is ranked 63rd on the list.

The Heavens Declare the Glory of God.

–SIGN 12–

LEO THE LION

The Prophetic Promise: The Lion of the Tribe of Judah Will Utterly Destroy the Enemy and Ultimately Rule over All.

They shall walk after the LORD He shall roar like a lion.

HOSEA 11:10

So we finally get to the end of the story! Leo is the book of Revelation written in the heavens! The great climax of this redemption story is the most dramatic of all signs in the heavens. Supported by its three minor constellations—Hydra, the Serpent being destroyed; Crater, the Cup of God's wrath poured out on the enemy; and Corvus, the Bird of prey devouring at the Valley of Armageddon—we see what Leo is all about.

Looking Up

The Hebrew name of the sign is Arieh, which means—you guessed it—"the Lion." It is not a tame lion. *Arieh* is the word used for "devouring its prey." Leo is pictured with His feet over the head of Hydra, the great Serpent, about to destroy it, just like foretold in Genesis at the fall of Adam and Eve in Genesis 3:15.

The brightest star marks the heart of the Lion. Its ancient name is Regulus, which means "treading under foot."

The next brightest star is in the tip of the tail, and this speaks of Jesus being the First and the Last. This is the picture of the end of Revelation where Jesus says,

*I am the Alpha and the Omega, the First
and the Last, the Beginning and the End.*

REVELATION 22:13 NIV

This star is named Denebola, "the Judge or the Lord who comes forward." The star in the mane is called Al Giebha, which means "the exalted One." Another star has the name Minchir al Asad, "the Lion is punishing." Deneb Aleced, "the coming judge who seizes," is another notable star in Leo. And another is Al Dafera (Arabic), meaning "the enemy is put down." Finally, Sarcam (Hebrew), which means "the joining," is the star Bullinger thinks is the point where the two ends of the Zodiac circle join.

So you understand how the story ends. The good guy wins and He wins big! Jesus the Messiah will put down and shamefully destroy all works of darkness. Paul put it this way:

> *Then comes the end, when He delivers the kingdom to
> God the Father, when He puts an end to all rule and all
> authority and power. For He must reign till He has put
> all enemies under His feet. The last enemy that will be
> destroyed is death. For "He has put all things under His
> feet." But when He says "all things are put under Him," it
> is evident that He who put all things under Him is excepted.*

1 CORINTHIANS 15:24-27

Leo is the book of Revelation written in the heavens, and Revelation is a book about the majesty of Jesus. He doesn't come the second time the way He came the first time. He doesn't show up as a 6-pound Jewish baby boy. There is nothing vulnerable about Him in this picture. He is invincible and unable to be defeated. God's people have nothing to fear because He is victorious!

> *And one of the elders said to me, "Weep*
> *no more; behold, the Lion of the tribe of*
> *Judah, the Root of David, has conquered...."*

REVELATION 5:5 ESV

Even so, come quickly, Lord Jesus, come quickly!

Star Party

- Leo is a highly recognizable constellation, as it is one of the few constellations that resemble its namesake. It is fairly easy to find because the "pointer stars" of the Big Dipper point to Leo.

- Leo lies between Cancer to the west and Virgo to the east.

- Leo is best seen in April at 9 p.m. local time.

- The brightest star in the constellation is Regulus, which has a surface temperature more than twice that of the Sun.

- Regulus, a blue-white beauty of a star, is the only first-magnitude star to sit squarely on the ecliptic— Earth's orbital plane projected onto the constellations of the Zodiac. It is 77 light-years distant from Earth.

- Seventy-seven is the number for the Church, and this is who the heart of the King beats for—the redeemed and His bride!

- There are 77 generations of Adam to the Christ according to the evangelist Luke (Luke 3:23-38).

- The word *church* is found in the Bible 77 times.

- The term *house of God* is found in the Bible 77 times.

- The word *garden* is found 77 times.

- The word *refuge* is found 77 times.

- The number 50, meaning *those set free,* is used 77 times in the Bible.

- The verb phrase *to forgive* is also in the Bible 77 times.

- The verb phrase *to feed* is used 77 times in the NRSC Bible.

- The celestial wonder Haley's Comet comes back into view from Earth every 77 years. It is a sign in the heavens that represents a word for the Church.

The Heavens Declare the Glory of God.

Those who are wise shall shine
Like the brightness of the firmament,
And those who turn many to righteousness
Like the stars forever and ever.

DANIEL 12:3

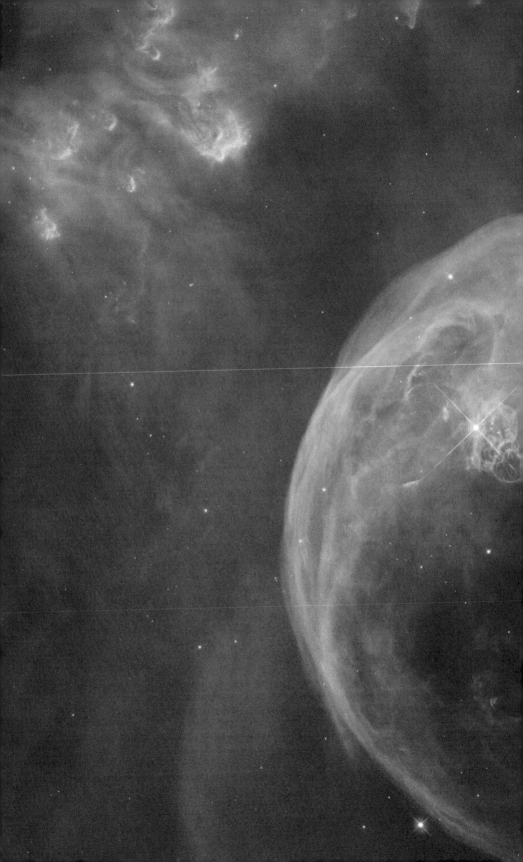

FOUR

These Are the Things Most People See

Familiar stars and what God is speaking through them

People learn to call certain stars certain things from the people they live life with. They see starry patterns in the heavens and they recall them accordingly. There are some that are just plain rockstars, and it seems everybody celebrates them in one way or another. This chapter will look at some of the most famous stars and constellations throughout the heavens. We should not be surprised at the volume at which they declare God's amazing message. Let's take a look.

Polaris: The North Star

The 50th-brightest star at 430 light-years away

The Story of Jesus on His Throne

He sits enthroned above the circle of the earth...

Isaiah 40:22 NIV

All the stories, all the constellations and all the drama circle one star—Polaris, known as the North Star. If you can't find any other star, you must be able to find the North Star. It's the star that gladdens the heart of every lost traveler.

For thousands of years, people could trek across the great desert, and 500 years ago, voyagers sailed the Atlantic, simply by spotting the North Star. It's the true star of navigation. If you learn how to see the North Star, you will never be lost again, and there will always be hope in your darkness. Do you see the picture? It's all about King Jesus sitting on His throne waiting to bring His lost sheep home. That's why all the other stars circle Polaris. The entire northern sky wheels around this star the same way the cherubim and the 24 elders circle the throne in Revelation chapter 4.

The Throne Chapter

There is actually a chapter in the Bible that theologians call "The Throne Chapter" that gives us in writing what Polaris gives us in symbol. John writes in Revelation 4:2:

> *Immediately I was in the Spirit; and behold, a throne was standing in heaven, and One sitting on the throne.*

John saw a throne "standing in heaven." That throne symbolizes the sovereign authority to rule. Apparently, the number 14 and the throne of Jesus are connected because the word *throne* is mentioned 14 times in this one chapter, and 14 more times in all other books.

As I pointed out in the second edition of my book *Numbers That Preach,* the number 14 is connected to God's sovereignty throughout the generations.

- Speaking of a great read, you should go to bible.org and look up *A Glimpse of His Glory*, by Pastor Keith Kreel. In a sermon, he writes this:

In Revelation chapter 4, John records that he saw "One sitting on the throne." The word "sitting" describes the position of a king who is actively reigning. For example, if a politician is "seated," he is said to be in office. If an unelected official is put out of office, he is said to be "unseated." John sees God "seated," meaning He is actively exercising the duties of His executive office, administering over the affairs of His creation.

So in the Kingdom, Polaris represents Jesus sitting, ruling, reigning and in total control. When He rules over you, you are never lost. Right now, He doesn't lead and guide everyone—only those who seek Him and find Him. Polaris is always there, but not always recognized. So it is with Jesus, and that's why the world is still lost.

The Forest and the Trees

The thing about the North Star is that you would never know it was there unless you were willing to look for it. Though it can be seen even through the light of big cities, it gets lost in myriad stars in the sky. It's not the brightest or the most beautiful, but it humbly sits in the heavens as the single-most important star, and the one that all others point to. It doesn't boast about itself at all.

It's the perfect picture of Jesus; always there, always in the center of everything, but easily dismissed and not recognized by the huge majority of people who occasionally look up. At first, Polaris just looks like any other star. When I first point out the North Star to people who have never seen it, they tend to be a bit disappointed at its appearance.

"What? Really?!" they say. This very much reminds me of Jesus as easily dismissed, but with severe consequences.

Is not this the carpenter's son? Is not His
mother called Mary? And are not his brothers
James and Joseph and Simon and Judas?

MATTHEW 13:55

Like one from whom people hide their faces he
was despised, and we held him in low esteem.

ISAIAH 53:3 NIV

There are times when the most significant is not the most

celebrated. Jesus and Polaris are the same in this respect. However, one who is willing, can gain a trained eye to both spot Him and celebrate Him.

Star Light, Star Bright

Most people assume the North Star would be the brightest star. They are badly mistaken. Polaris is the 50th-brightest star. There are 49 other stars easier to spot. It's not hard to find this one, but you must be intentional. Though ranked number 50, 50 is the number for Jubilee and that's a prophetic declaration. On the 50th year according to the book of Leviticus, slaves and prisoners would be freed, debts would be forgiven and the mercies of God would be particularly manifest. That's what happens when you see 50.

> *And you shall consecrate the fiftieth year, and proclaim*
> *liberty throughout all the land to all its inhabitants. It*
> *shall be a Jubilee for you; and each of you shall return to*
> *his possession, and each of you shall return to his family*

LEVITICUS 25:10

It is no coincidence that the one star that all others circle would be the 50th-brightest in the heavens! When you see Jesus and your life revolves around Him, you are no longer a slave to sin. Your debts are forgiven and God's mercy is made manifest in your life. You are brought back into the family—no longer a slave and no longer lost.

Far Away and Super Bright

Polaris is a yellow super-giant that shines at the luminosity of 2,500 suns. Astronomers estimate Polaris' distance at 430 light-years away from us.

Since we are talking about how Polaris represents Jesus on the throne, I think it is right for us to look at what the Bible says in Revelation:

And He who sat there was like a jasper and a
sardius stone in appearance; and there was a rainbow
around the throne, in appearance like an emerald.

REVELATION 4:3

I know this is Revelation, but did you know the numbers in the Bible go with the numbers science has provided? Revelation 4:3 and the light distance of Polaris—430—have the same numbers: 43. It is no coincidence that the star which represents the throne, and the Bible verse which describes the throne, have the same numbers. God is behind the declaring of both of them.

I think it's amazing that both Exodus 4:30 and Acts 4:30 speak of miraculous "signs." There is no doubt that Polaris, the star that represents Jesus on His throne, was put there as a sign in the heavens at 430 light-years away.

... and let them be for signs.

GENESIS 1:14

But I also want to tell you it grieves God when people are lost. God has a holy hatred for the way people get off course and stumble in the darkness. He wants so badly for you and I to go out of our way to seek Him and to find Him. He doesn't want our ships to hit the reef, or for us to miss the oasis in the desert. This is why Polaris is there every single night. In the book of Ephesians, marked by the same number as Polaris, the Bible says:

And do not grieve the Holy Spirit of God, by
whom you were sealed for the day of redemption.

Ephesians 4:30

Looking Up: The Message Polaris Preaches

- Everything circles the throne (Revelation 7:11)
- You only see Him if you are willing to seek Him (Proverbs 8:17)
- Someone else has to point Him out to you (Romans 10:14)
- He doesn't look the way you think (Philippians 2:7)
- Once you see Him, you will never be lost again (Luke 15:1-10)
- Once you see Him, you are set free (John 8:36)
- It grieves God that men do not see Him and remain lost (Ezekiel 6:9-10)

The heavens declare the glory of God
and this is what the heavens declare
through Polaris, the North Star.

The Big Dipper: Ursa Major

Seven stars that are part of a much bigger constellation

The Church Who Points the Way to Jesus

Looking unto Jesus, the author and finisher of our faith....

Hebrews 12:2

Located in the northern sky at any time of year, you can find the Big Dipper. Mostly because, like its name boasts, it's really big and the seven-star wonder is especially bright. It has a very important role in the heavens; it points us to the North Star and makes Polaris easy to find. In Acts, Philip asked a mighty warrior if he knew who the Messiah was. The warrior replied:

> *And he said, "How can I, unless someone guides me?"*
> *And he asked Philip to come up and sit with him.*

Acts 8:31

I'm just going to cut to the chase and tell you that the Big Dipper is actually a picture of the seven stars in the book of Revelation. They represent the Church, and our job is to point people to the One everything rotates around—Jesus.

Americana

The Big Dipper constellation is one that people tend to look for and Americans are extremely fond of.

"Look!" we like to say, pointing at Orion. "It's the Big Dipper."

The Big Dipper is not Orion as a lot of people think. It's not even an actual constellation—it's just the brightest part of a constellation. To go a step further, it isn't even a dipper! The Greeks call it a giant bear, but to tell you the truth, it's not a bear either. How many great bears have you ever seen with a giant tail? None!

There's a lot of confusion about the Big Dipper, and I believe it's because the dipper represents the Church. For 2,000 years, there has been endless confusion on the identity of the body of Christ. It only makes sense that our picture in the heavens would have the same controversy. Let's just make it simple why there are so many names and different ideas about what these seven stars represent. This is fun stuff to me.

Manifest Destiny

President Theodore Roosevelt described it as "the great leap Westward." Folks painted their wagons and took off for the promise of something better out West under a wandering star. Hillbilly children and frontier parents didn't sleep all that well at night. Their wagon trains, sometimes consisting of hundreds and hundreds of people, were dotted with crying babies, singing families, coughing sick people and lots of night watchmen wondering if the noise they heard in the dark was an Indian or some monster yet to be discovered.

One thing every pioneer family had in common was a wagon. Though they all had 2,000 pounds of different possessions, every wagon had a wooden water barrel. Located at the back and positioned low for easy access, people would reach for it often as they walked over 20 miles a day through treacherous territory. Every child used the big ladle, long enough to reach the bottom of the barrel, and I imagine they reached for it a dozen times a day or more.

So envision with me a crisp, fall night—the sound of crickets and a crackling fire. No TV or radio, just a daddy, a mama, and a couple of kids literally in the middle of nowhere with nothing to do but look at the stars above and dream of a life they might have on the other side of the mountains. The stars they saw were every bit as bright back then as they are at a planetarium today. It's in this setting that one of the kids points to the seven bright stars in the North American sky and says, "Look, Pa, it's the Big Dipper."

Trail bosses, wagon masters, scouts and guides went back to Independence, Missouri, pointed at the same seven stars and called it the same thing as thousands more families hit the Oregon Trail. It made sense to everybody. The star formation looked like a Big Dipper to them. All pioneers and trail bosses knew that by keeping the Big Dipper and the North Star it pointed to on their right shoulder, they were always headed west.

Finding Your Way

The Big Dipper and Polaris also play an important part in the story of the Underground Railroad, which helped slaves escape the southern states before the Civil War.

Slaves were taught a folk song called "Follow the Drinking Gourd." It actually showed them how to find the Big Dipper and the North Star. What was called the Big Dipper out West, was called the Drinking Gourd down South. The brilliant tune was a secret code that gave directions for the escape route from Alabama and Mississippi to Canada in the north. It was a long and fearful journey, but they would comfort each other at night by telling which way was north by the location of Polaris, which they could find by the pointer stars of the Drinking Gourd.

The Heavenly Navigator

The Big Dipper has always pointed people to freedom from slavery and rescue from being lost—not because it's a spoon, or a gourd, or even a bear, but because prophetically, it is a picture of the body of Christ.

There are two pointer stars and the brightest star is named Dubhe, which means "a herd of animals or a flock." This star gives the real meaning of the whole constellation. The other pointer star is a Hebrew name, Merach, and it means "the flock." You got it—it's a flock of sheep! It's a herd of animals dependent upon a shepherd.

The Big Dipper shows us what the seven stars, or the Church is supposed to do. No matter how big or attractive we may be, our job is to point lost people to rescue and slaves to freedom. The Father pointed people to Jesus. The Holy Spirit points people to Jesus. John the Baptist pointed people to Jesus. The Bible points people to Jesus. The New Testament Christians pointed people to Jesus. Even Jesus pointed people to Himself.

> *Then Jesus declared, "I am the bread of life.*
> *Whoever comes to me will never go hungry, and*
> *Whoever believes in me will never be thirsty."*

> JOHN 6:35 NIV

It just goes to show that we, the Church—the body of Jesus—should be pointing people to Jesus! The Church is not the answer. Jesus is the answer, and the Church is supposed to be proof of that. We need to be constantly saying what Amos once said:

> *Seek him who created the Seven Stars....*

> AMOS 5:8 KJV

You and I, as His sheep, are supposed to be a prophetic compass. How we live as His sheep actually matters more than we realize. If we are off course, we can't lead others who are off course.

*The integrity of the upright will guide them, but
the perversity of the unfaithful will destroy them.*

PROVERBS 11:3

It's a sad night when you are lost in the wilderness and the
light of the seven stars of the Big Dipper cannot be seen. Let's all
remember that as a true congregation of believers, we need to
remain as faithful as the stars Dubhe, Merak, Phecda, Megrez,
Alioth, Mizar and Alkaid.

The Names of the Stars, Their Meanings and Numbers

- Dubhe: "a herd of animals, or a flock," is located 124
  light-years away.

- Merck (Hebrew): "the flock," located 79 light-years
  away.

- Phecda: "visited, guarded, or numbered, as a flock,"
  located 84 light-years away.

- Megrez: "base of the tail or follows behind," located
  58 light-years away.

- Alioth: "a she goat," located 81 light-years away.

- Mizar: "separate or small," located 78 light-years
  away.

- Alkaid: "the assembled," located 101 light-years away.

The brightest star in the Big Dipper, Dubhe, is 124 light-
years away. This makes me think of the Psalm with the same
number. They both shout the responsibility we have, just like
the Big Dipper, to point to the One who saves us.

Let Israel now say—
"If it had not been the Lord who was on
our side, When men rose up against us,
Then they would have swallowed us alive, When
their wrath was kindled against us; Then the waters
would have overwhelmed us, The stream would
have gone over our soul; Then the swollen waters
Would have gone over our soul." Blessed be the Lord,
Who has not given us as prey to their teeth.
Our soul has escaped as a bird from the snare of the
fowlers;[a] The snare is broken, and we have escaped.
Our help is in the name of the
Lord, Who made heaven and earth.

Psalm 124

One Last Note on the Big Dipper

In the book of Job (9:9; 38:31-32), the Big Dipper is mentioned under the name of Ash. God is having a great one-sided conversation with brother Job, which is kind of like God prequalifying Job for the answer to the "Let's see if you can handle the whys of life" question.

If Job can answer some very fundamental questions about nature, he qualifies for the answer to the much bigger "why" question.

God asks Job, "Can you guide Ash and her offspring?" The answer is obviously, "No."

This conversation between Job and God happened about 4,000 years ago. God was talking about what you and I refer to today as the Big Dipper. Sometimes it's translated as "Arcturus and his sons," and sometimes as "the Bear with her train," or "the bear and her babies or sons." So it turns out the last three dots are not the tail of the bear, but the ones she is responsible for leading to the one guiding her—Polaris—and that's Jesus seated on His throne as we have already discussed. We have a tremendous responsibility to the next generation of believers to follow Christ and to point them to Jesus (Polaris).

Looking Up: The Message the Big Dipper Preaches

- The ones who circle the throne on high are His sheep (Psalm 107:41)

- People look to us to point the way to Him (Acts 8:31)

- The Church is to be a heavenly compass (1 Corinthians 2:11)

- The Church is responsible for following and for those who follow (John 21:17)

This is what the heavens declare through The Big Dipper.

Orion

A winter constellation made of 78 stars

Jesus is the Light and Hope of the World

*Arise, shine; For your light has come!
And the glory of the Lord is risen upon you.*

Isaiah 60:1

As one of the brightest and best-known constellations in the sky, Orion stands out as Heaven's rockstar. You cannot ignore him. You cannot deny him. When it's time for him to show up, you know it. Orion is beautiful, majestic and seen by everyone who looks up in the winter. As a supporting cast member for the sign of Taurus, the job of Orion is to let us know that the One coming back and busting through everything, does not just come back with the momentum of the bull. He is also "One altogether lovely."

His mouth is most sweet, yes, he is altogether lovely. This is my beloved, and this is my friend, o daughters of Jerusalem!

SONG OF SOLOMON 5:16

For so the Lord has commanded us: "I have set you as a light to the Gentiles, That you should be for salvation to the ends of the earth."

ACTS 13:47

The best time to see Orion is in late January at 9:00 p.m., but you can actually see him long before that and way afterward.

Orion Means "Light"

A long time ago, Orion was spelled Oarion, which comes from the Hebrew root word for "light." Others called him Ur-ana, which means "the light of Heaven." This is Jesus in His grandest form showing us who He conquers, why He conquers and how.

I have come as a light into the world, that whoever believes in Me should not abide in darkness.

JOHN 12:46

As long as I am in the world, I am the light of the world.

JOHN 9:5

That was the true Light which gives
light to every man coming into the world.

JOHN 1:9

Make no mistake: the sky is not falling; the Kingdom is coming!

The Babylonians called Orion "MULSIPA.ZI.AN.NA," and that means "the heavenly shepherd" of "the true shepherd of God." Here Jesus has arrived and His sheep will lack for nothing from this day forward.

The Lord is my shepherd; I shall not want.

PSALM 23:1

As He returns like a shepherd, He will divide the sheep from the goats.

All the nations will be gathered before Him,
and He will separate them one from another,
as a shepherd divides his sheep from the goats.

MATTHEW 25:32

It's interesting to note that Mitaka, the star furthest right in Orion's famous belt, is an ancient word that means "dividing." He is definitely going to do His job!

Let's Look at the Stars

The brightest star in Orion is located in his left foot. It is called Rigel, which means "the foot that crushes."

*His feet were like fine brass, as if refined in a
furnace, and His voice as the sound of many waters.*

REVELATION 1:15

*And He put all things under His feet, and gave
Him to be head over all things to the church.*

EPHESIANS 1:22

When Jesus comes back, His feet are as brass, a symbol
of judgment (Revelation 2:18). The Bible goes on to say that
He stomps the enemy out, the way that Lucille Ball danced on
grapes back in 1956.

*And the winepress was trampled outside the city, and
blood came out of the winepress, up to the horses'
bridles, for one thousand six hundred furlongs.*

REVELATION 14:20

*Now out of His mouth goes a sharp sword, that with
it He should strike the nations. And He Himself will
rule them with a rod of iron. He Himself treads the
winepress of the fierceness and wrath of Almighty God.*

REVELATION 19:15

The "Battle Hymn of the Republic" sang about "the grapes
of wrath." So did Elvis in "American Trilogy." John Steinbeck
wrote a book about those infamous grapes in 1939, which won
a Pulitzer Prize. John Ford made a movie about them and won
the Oscar for best director.

I am telling you, God will bless you if you start writing or
singing about how Jesus is going to stomp out all of our enemies.

A long time before John even had a revelation of it, the heavens declared it through Orion and Rigel.

Facts About Rigel

Overall, Rigel is about 40,000 times brighter than our local star, the Sun. Earth would need to be about 200 times further away, or about five times as far as Pluto, to bear life in orbit around Rigel.

Even then, the light would be a weird bluish light. Rigel is 66,000 times more powerful than the Sun, has 17 times more mass, and 70 times the width of our Sun. Rigel is the seventh-brightest star in the heavens. It is a blue supergiant star, and is 773 light-years from Earth. In other words, the light you see from Rigel on any given winter night, started on its journey a least 250 years before Columbus stumbled upon the outskirts of North America.

It's Show Time

The next brightest star is called Betelgeuse. It is pronounced "Beatle Juice," just like the Tim Burton movie. Betelgeuse means "the coming of the BRANCH."

> *But who can endure the day of His coming?*
> *And who can stand when He appears? For He*
> *is like a refiner's fire and like launderers' soap.*

> MALACHI 3:2

> *There shall come forth a Rod from the stem of*
> *Jesse, And a Branch shall grow out of his roots.*

> ISAIAH 11:1

Yes, before that was ever written prophetically in the Bible, it was prophetically written in the heavens, in the names of the stars which God loves to name.

Betelgeuse Facts

A red supergiant, which is a rare thing—we know of only about 200 in our galaxy—it's hard to imagine how big this thing actually is. If this star were our Sun, we would be in big trouble. You know how far away our Sun is from us? Something like 92.96 million miles away, and it takes light from the Sun eight minutes and 20 seconds to reach us. Light travels at 186,282 miles per second and that's hauling the mail! Ok, so you need to know that the Sun is a long way away, big in our sky and extremely hot. So our Sun has to be monstrous.

Betelgeuse is so much bigger than our Sun, if it were placed where our Sun is, it wouldn't be far away at all. In fact, it would not be away at all. We would be deep within the inside of the star itself because Betelgeuse is much bigger around than our rotation around the Sun! It would go all the way into Jupiter's orbit, and Jupiter is three times farther away from us than the Sun is.

When the two planets are at their closest point, the distance to Jupiter is 365 million miles. At its farthest, the gas giant lies 601 million miles away from us. Betelgeuse is bigger than you can possibly imagine and it is 642 light-years away.

Isaiah, using the same prophetic numbers, says what Orion is all about—in representing Jesus:

> *As fire burns brushwood, as fire causes water to boil—*
> *To make Your name known to Your adversaries,*
> *That the nations may tremble at Your presence!*

ISAIAH 64:2

The light of the world is coming back soon and the nations will tremble! Before that was prophetically written in the Bible, it was prophetically written in the heavens in the constellation Orion.

When Jesus comes back, the light of the world—Orion—comes back.

Bellatrix

Bellatrix is the third-brightest star in the constellation Orion, 5-degrees right of the red giant Betelgeuse. It is the 27th-brightest star in the night sky and 250 light-years away.

Jim Kaler, Professor Emeritus of Astronomy, University of Illinois says,

> If constellations could talk, they might well shout "unfair" at great Orion, one of only four constellations to have two FIRST magnitude stars (the others being the Southern Cross, the Centaur, and Canis Major, Orion's Hunting Dog). Moreover, it also has the fourth, seventh, and eighth-brightest SECOND magnitude stars. The brightest of these, Bellatrix, magnitude 1.64, follows immediately behind Castor (in Gemini), Gacrux (in the cross), and Shaula (in Scorpio).

Bellatrix, which means "quickly coming," is what the Bible is talking about when Jesus comes back to defeat His enemies.

> *Repent, or else I will come to you quickly and will*
> *fight against them with the sword of My mouth.*
>
> Revelation 2:16

*Behold, I am coming quickly! Blessed is he who
keeps the words of the prophecy of this book.*

REVELATION 22:7

*And behold, I am coming quickly, and My reward is
with Me, to give to every one according to his work.*

REVELATION 22:12

You should also see this theme in Revelation 2:5, Revelation 11:14, and Revelation 3:11. This is what our response to the proclamation of Bellatrix should be:

*I Am Coming Quickly He who testifies
to these things says, "Surely I am coming
quickly." Amen. Even so, come, Lord Jesus!*

REVELATION 22:20

Behold, Orion!

Orion the conqueror is a picture of a "warrior prince"and "the Light of the World" with his left foot positioned over the head of the enemy. His world-famous belt of three beautiful stars has a sword hanging off of it. In Orion's right hand, he holds a mighty club, which is the rod for his enemies. In his left hand, he holds the skin of the roaring lion whom he has defeated. He is showing off his trophy and displaying the spoils of war. He is undefeatable, unstoppable and undeniable. Orion is Heaven's greatest rockstar.

Orion's Belt

*Orion stands wrapped about with a belt of truth.
Stand therefore, having girded your waist with truth....*

EPHESIANS 6:14

The three stars on Orion's Belt are famous in cultures everywhere. However, they are most famous in Egypt. There, the ancient astronomers lined up the three great pyramids with the three brightest stars in Orion's belt. They were looking for the truth and He's still wanting to set them free. Look it up!

In the Bible, the belt is represented as truth.

- Al Nitak: located 815 light-years away, it means "the wounded One" (Isaiah 53:5, Genesis 3:15)

- Al Nilam: located 1,350 light-years away. The buckle of the belt is loosely translated as "string of pearls," but it comes from a root word meaning "to honor" and "being exalted" (Psalm 21:5; Psalm 66:2; Psalm 96:6; Revelation 5:12; Revelation 5:13)

> *You are worthy, O Lord, To receive glory and*
> *honor and power; For You created all things,*
> *And by Your will they exist and were created.*

> REVELATION 4:11

- Mitaka: located 916 light-years away, it is an ancient word that means "dividing" (Psalms 29:7, Isaiah 51:15, Matthew 25:32)

> *And God saw the light, that it was good;*
> *and God divided the light from the darkness.*

> GENESIS 1:4

Orion's Sword

The center of Orion's sword is the great Orion Nebula. It's the only nebula you can see with the naked eye. Located over 1,300 light-years away, scientists say it's a stellar nursery where new stars are being born. According to modern astronomers, the Orion Nebula is an enormous cloud of gas and dust, one of many in our Milky Way Galaxy, and it is making new stars even as you are reading this.

The dark-sky aficionado, Stephen James O'Meara, described the nebula as "… angel's breath against a frosted sky."

…the sword of the Spirit, which is the word of God….

EPHESIANS 6:17

On the handle of the sword, and pictured on all the old star maps, is supposed to be the head of a lamb. This is proof of who He actually is. He is the Lamb who was slain.

Saying with a loud voice: "Worthy is the Lamb who
was slain To receive power and riches and wisdom,
And strength and honor and glory and blessing!"

REVELATION 5:12

The next star, in the left shoulder, is called Bellatrix, which means "quickly coming, or swiftly destroying." The name of the fourth star, one of the three in the belt, carries us back to the old story that this glorious One was once humbled and that His heel was once bruised. It's name is Al Nitak, "the wounded One." Similarly, the star located in the right leg, is called Saiph, which means "bruised."

Looking Up: Amazing Messages That Orion Preaches

- Jesus is the Light of the World: the name Orion (John 12:46)

- Jesus is coming back quickly: the star Bellatrix (Revelation 22:7)

- He will stomp on His enemies and put them under His feet (Revelation 14:20)

- He will divide the goats from the sheep: the Star Mitaka (Matthew 25:32)

- This is the truth: Orion's belt (Ephesians 6:14)

- A sword will come from His mouth against the nations: Orion's sword (Revelation 19:15)

- He will ultimately defeat death and take away tears

And God will wipe away every tear from their eyes; there shall be no more death, nor sorrow, nor crying. There shall be no more pain, for the former things have passed away.

REVELATION 21:4

When Orion rises, Scorpio disappears. Orion and Scorpio can never be seen in the same sky. The light of the world (as represented through Betelgeuse) literally chases away the heart of darkness (as represented through Antares and Scorpio).

Cassiopeia: When Jesus Comes Back, His Bride Is Righteous

"...Come, I will show you the bride, the Lamb's wife."
And he carried me away in the Spirit to a great and high
mountain, and showed me the great city, the holy Jerusalem,
descending out of heaven from God, having the glory of God.

REVELATION 21:9-11

Cassiopeia looks like a W, a 3 and finally an M as she makes her way around the North Star. She is seen as a queen on her throne, but she is upside down when she first rises above the horizon in the east. Then, dramatically, as her lover and glorious redeemer, Orion, arises, she is made righteous at His appearing. She is right side up as Orion climbs into the same sky.

Finally, there is laid up for me the crown of
righteousness, which the Lord, the righteous Judge,
will give to me on that Day, and not to me only
but also to all who have loved His appearing.

2 TIMOTHY 4:8

This is what the heavens declare through Orion, and it is AWESOME!

Sirius: The Dog Star

The brightest star in all the heavens at 8.6 light-years distant

Jesus: The Hope and Ruler over Gentile Nations

The Gentiles shall come to your light,
And kings to the brightness of your rising.

ISAIAH 60:3

While Orion is the brightest constellation, Sirius is the brightest of all stars. It's the big dog. The sire of all sirs. The brightest and biggest. It's the Elvis to rock 'n roll and the Garth

Brooks to country music. This is Sirius, and it's part of the constellation known as Canis Major, or "the big dog."

The Persians called him "the chieftain of the east." Other ancients called this star "the Prince of the heavenly host." So it makes sense that the next brightest star, Mizram, means "the ruling Prince." This is Jesus in His majesty portrayed to the Gentile nations as a much bigger dog than they.

...A leader and commander for the people.

ISAIAH 55:4

This is the truth Orion's Belt points to. Simply draw a line through Orion's Belt to the left and it points to Sirius. It is roughly eight times as far from the Belt, as the Belt is wide. There is none brighter. His brightness is greater. There is none more glorious and He will not be out-shined by any Gentile nation.

And then the lawless one will be revealed, whom the
Lord will consume with the breath of His mouth
and destroy with the brightness of His coming.

2 THESSALONIANS 2:8

Dyslexic Dog

The whole "dog thing" comes from the same idea where we get the term Big Dog. It means the biggest, the baddest, the one with the most authority. Among the Jews, to be called a dog is a demeaning term reserved for Gentiles and those who are not within the covenant (Proverbs 22:16, 1 Samuel 17:43, 2 Samuel 9:8, Proverbs 26:11, Matthew 7:6). For Jesus to be seen as the Big Dog of Heaven literally means to be glorified as ruler over all Gentile nations.

Every Color of Every Gentile People in the World

Although white to blue-white in color, Sirius might be called a rainbow star, as it often flickers with many colors. It flickers because the columns of air its light passes through before we see it. Some hot and some cold, but all of it changing the color of the light as it darts through space toward us. This is a symbol of covenant.

> *I set My rainbow in the cloud, and it shall be for the sign of the covenant between Me and the earth.*
>
> GENESIS 9:13

This is what He is offering to the Gentile nations who love His appearing: covenant (2 Timothy 4:8).

Every Eye Shall See Him

Sirius can be seen from every location on Earth at some time throughout the year. You can't help but notice Sirius because it is more than three times brighter than the next brightest star.

> *Behold, He is coming with clouds, and every eye will see Him, even they who pierced Him. And all the tribes of the earth will mourn because of Him. Even so, Amen.*
>
> REVELATION 1:7

From There to Here

Sirius is located exactly 8.6 light-years from Earth. There is a biblical message in that number.

*You have made him to have dominion over the works
of Your hands; You have put all things under his feet.*

PSALM 8:6

*Listen, for I will speak of excellent things, And
from the opening of my lips will come right things.*

PROVERBS 8:6

*For to be carnally minded is death, but
to be spiritually minded is life and peace.*

ROMANS 8:6

*But now He has obtained a more excellent ministry,
inasmuch as He is also Mediator of a better
covenant, which was established on better promises.*

HEBREWS 8:6

*So the seven angels who had the seven
trumpets prepared themselves to sound.*

REVELATION 8:6

Looking Up: The Message Sirius the Big Dog Preaches

- Jesus is the King of Kings and Lord of Lords (1 Timothy 6:15, Revelation 17:14, Revelation 19:16)
- Every eye will see Him (Revelation 1:7)
- He will rule and reign over all Gentile nations (Isaiah 60:3)
- He comes with covenant (Genesis 9:13)

- Jesus is salvation to the Gentiles (Acts 13:48)

*This is what the heavens declare
through Sirius the Dog Star.*

The Summer Triangle

An astronomical asterism involving three stars:
Altair, Deneb and Vega

Jesus Christ Fallen, Risen and Coming Back Again

> *If anyone speaks, let him speak as the oracles of God.*
> *If anyone ministers, let him do it as with the ability*
> *which God supplies, that in all things God may*
> *be glorified through Jesus Christ, to whom belong*
> *the glory and the dominion forever and ever. Amen.*

1 PETER 4:11

During the summer months, the Summer Triangle star formation lights the sky from dusk until dawn. It consists of three bright stars: Vega in the constellation Lyra, Deneb in the constellation Cygnus, and Altair in the constellation Aquila. Buckle your seat belts because this is seriously, or Sirius-ly, awesome!

Lyra, the Harp and the Cool Blue Star, Vega

As dusk deepens into darkness on a warm June or July night, look eastward for a sparkling blue-white star whose name is Vega. Reigning at the apex of the celebrated Summer Triangle, Vega overwhelms as the brightest of it's three glorious stars. Vega is an amazing star and its name means "He shall be exalted." Vega and Lyra, the Harp, represent praise and worship, and this is a cosmic hallelujah!

*Sing to the Lord with the harp, With
the harp and the sound of a psalm.*

PSALM 98:5

Lyra is one of the three minor constellations which back up the story God speaks through Sagittarius. This is the triumphant song that you sing after you see King Jesus on His big white horse with His bow in His hand.

*You will make ready Your arrows
on Your string toward their faces.
Be exalted, O Lord, in Your own strength!
We will sing and praise Your power.*

PSALM 21:12-13

Viva Las Vega!

Because Vega is the fifth-brightest star and is 25 (5x5) light-years away, it is a star associated with the grace of God. Is there any greater reason to give God praise?

Examples of five representing grace:

- The word *adoption* is found five times in the Bible.

- The various forms of the word *righteous* are found 555 times in the Bible.

- God established His covenant with Abraham by five sacrifices: a bull, sheep, goat, dove, and pigeon (Genesis 15:9).

- Jesus received five wounds while on the cross as the perfect sacrifice.

*For by grace are ye saved through faith; and
that not of yourselves: it is the gift of God....*

EPHESIANS 2:8 KJV

Five at a Coming-Out Party

Israel came out of Egypt ranked in fives (Exodus 13:18), proving it was God's power that freed them. The number five is marked all over the Exodus, preaching there's no bondage God's grace cannot bring you out of.

Five at a Rock Concert

David picked up five smooth stones when coming against Goliath, preaching that it was by God's grace he would defeat the giant.

*Then said David to the Philistine, Thou comest to me
with a sword, and with a spear, and with a shield: but
I come to thee in the name of the LORD of hosts, the
God of the armies of Israel, whom thou hast defied.*

1 SAMUEL 17:45 KJV

Grace is the power to overcome every enemy.

Five on a Soapbox

Paul writes of speaking clearly in the church and the Holy Spirit marks it with the number five:

*Yet in the church I had rather speak five words with my
understanding, that by my voice I might teach others
also, than ten thousand words in an unknown tongue.*

1 CORINTHIANS 14:19

It is by the grace of God that we speak and teach anything. Teaching and being teachable both come from the grace of Almighty God.

Five in an Oil Stick

The holy anointing oil was made of five ingredients (Exodus 30:23-25). This precious oil was the symbol of God's power to set things, and even people, apart for His purpose and use, and to mark them as His holy territory. For the Christian, God's anointing is on our life. It is still marked by the number five and grace.

> *For God hath not given us the spirit of fear; but of power, and of love, and of a sound mind. Be not thou therefore ashamed of the testimony of our Lord, nor of me his prisoner: but be thou partaker of the afflictions of the gospel according to the power of God; Who hath saved us, and called us with an holy calling, not according to our works, but according to his own purpose and grace, which was given us in Christ Jesus before the world began,*
>
> 2 TIMOTHY 1:7-9 KJV

Grace is the power to separate you for His use and call you holy. Grace is the God-given ability to not be afraid, but to walk in the spirit of power, love and a sound mind. I will take all He is willing to dish out! Pour it on me, Lord Jesus, and call me anointed!

Five Gone Swimming

The pool of Bethesda had five porches. It was there that a lame man was healed and made able to walk (John 5). This is a picture of the truth that, by God's grace, we walk in Jesus. Until He makes us able, we "have no man," as the brother proclaimed, to help us.

As ye have therefore received Christ
Jesus the Lord, so walk ye in him....

COLOSSIANS 2:6 KJV

You can't progress until you receive Jesus. He wants to give us the power to progress, especially in Him, but we are never going to find it outside of His grace.

The Cool Blue of Vega

Vega's distinctly blue color indicates a surface temperature of nearly 17,000 degrees Fahrenheit, making it about 7,000 degrees hotter than our Sun. Those are also prophetic numbers with the same theme—grace. Seventeen is the number for overcoming with victory. An example is the 17 promises to "Him who overcomes" in Revelation. Seven is the most prolific number in the Bible and represents spiritual perfection or the manifest power of the Spirit of God.

The Swan and Beyond

Next up in the Summer Triangle, we have two stars of prophetic importance: Cignus, the Swan, and the bright star Deneb. Deneb is located in the tail of the great swan and at the head of the Northern Cross. The Cross and Swan used to be called Tesark in the Denderah Zodiac and it means "here from afar," "here from a long way away" or "after a long time." It prophetically speaks of the return of Jesus Christ in full flight. Two of the Gospel writers describe this event in dramatic fashion:

For as the lightning comes from the east and flashes to
the west, so also will the coming of the Son of Man be.

MATTHEW 24:27

For as the lightning that flashes out of one part
under heaven shines to the other part under
heaven, so also the Son of Man will be in His day.

LUKE 17:24

Deneb: Light from Far Away

Deneb is one of the most distant stars you will see with your eye alone. That's because it's one of the most luminous stars in the Milky Way Galaxy. The exact distance to Deneb is unclear, with estimates ranging from about 1,425 light-years to perhaps as much as 7,000 light-years. The best estimates for Deneb's distance are those obtained by the Hipparcos Space Astrometry Mission in the 1990s. A simple calculation from initial Hipparcos data gives the figure of 3,230 light- years. At any estimated distance, Deneb is one of the farthest stars the unaided human eye can see. It is so far, the light that reaches the Earth today, started on its journey thousands of years ago.

Professor James Kaler, using the figure of 2,600 light-years as the distance, estimated a diameter 200 times greater than our Sun, and about a quarter of a million times brighter in visible light.

Deneb is the 20th-brightest star. It is 200 times bigger than our Sun. Twenty is the number for expectancy and waiting on the Lord. It's no wonder this constellation is connected with expecting Jesus to come back quickly.

Deneb being located in the tail of the Swan means "the Judge." Another star, SADR (Hebrew), in the body of the swan means "returning," and Al Bireo in the beak means "quickly." When you read all three stars in the order they are in the heavens, it says:

The Judge Is Returning—Quickly

Can you think of a judge who is coming quickly who used to be on a cross? That's what Cygnus, the Swan, is all about.

As a minor constellation in the sign of Aquarius, it is clear that this is the blessed hope of those who are born again and have the Spirit of God poured out upon us.

"The Wild Goose Chase"

This term first showed up in Shakespeare's Romeo and Juliet, although the meaning is different from how we know it today —namely a task that has no hope of succeeding or a pursuit for something unattainable. To Shakespeare, it suggested something else. The "wild goose chase" he was talking about was a 16th-century cross-country horse race.

The general idea was for horses to follow a lead rider at a distance, copying his route exactly. The lead would twist and turn to make the course tricky to follow, causing people to compare the race to wild geese flying in formation. But the British stole the term from the Scotts a thousand years earlier. The ancient Celts had a term for the Spirit of God called "An Geadh Glas" or "the wild goose." This term came about because they got a revelation from the sign of the cross in the heavens we are referring to now. They knew it represented God, and that they should follow Him and pursue Him!

The Judge who is returning quickly was identified to them as the message of Christianity, and it reached them in the fifth century. They already had a Celtic cross and they were ready to follow the wild goose! The next time you see a Celtic cross, know that the Celts already had a revelation, and their preacher was Cygnus the Swan!

I'm going to follow King Jesus and chase the wild goose from one adventure into another!

The Third Part of the Summer Triangle: Aquila, the Fallen Eagle

He is the picture a majestic creature from heaven, an eagle who has been shot down.

Altair, the brightest star in Aquila, is the 12th-brightest star, and therefore is connected with kingdom and government. Twelve marks when God is in control of something. That's why Jesus declared that He could call on the power of 12 legions of angels (Matthew 26:53). Other notable "12" facts supporting this are:

- The first recorded words of Jesus were at the age of 12.
- There were 12 baskets of fragments left over when Jesus miraculously fed the crowds of people.
- There are 12 sons of Jacob.
- There are 12 tribes of Israel.
- There are 12 disciples.
- There were 12 spies sent out by Moses in Numbers chapter 13.
- Elijah built an altar of 12 stones when he called fire down from Heaven (1 Kings 18:31-38).
- There are 12 months in a year because God rules over every year.
- There are 12 major constellations because God rules over all the heavens.

- There are 60 minutes in an hour (12 x 5) and 60 seconds in a minute, because God perfectly governs every nano moment that has ever been measured.

Altair is exactly 16.8 light-years away from Earth. The number 16 represents the love of God and eight represents new beginnings. So, 16.8 is another way of saying 888—the numerical value of the name JESUS! The numerical value of the name of Jesus as it is written in Greek is 888 (111 x 8), while the number of the anti-Christ, or the beast, is 666.

Iesous = 888

I (10) + e (8) + s (200) + o (70) + u (400) + s (200)

Altair means "the wounding" or in modern-day terms we might say "the beat down." Aquila is pictured as the death scene of King Jesus Himself. What's more, Altair is flanked by two other stars, Tarazed, which means "torn back" or "stripped back," and Alshain, which means "bright red" or "bleeding." Not only is this a prophetic picture of Jesus flanked by two thieves also being tortured on a cross, do you what those three stars are saying? The same as Isaiah 53:5:

> *But He was wounded for our transgressions* [Altair],
> *He was bruised for our iniquities* [Alshain];
> *The chastisement for our peace was upon Him,*
> *And by His stripes we are healed* [Tarazed].

The star in the lower wing is called Alcair, which means "the piercing."

For dogs have surrounded Me; the congregation of the wicked
has enclosed Me. They pierced My hands and My feet;

PSALM 22:16

This is also in Zechariah 12:10:

And I will pour on the house of David and on the
inhabitants of Jerusalem the Spirit of grace and
supplication; then they will look on Me whom they pierced.

And John 19:34:

But one of the soldiers pierced His side with a
spear, and immediately blood and water came out.
But one of the soldiers pierced His side with a
spear, and immediately blood and water came out.

So in the Summer Triangle we have the death, resurrection and return of the Lord Jesus Christ in full display through Altair, Vega, and Deneb. WOW!

Looking Up: The Message the Summer Triangle Preaches

- The story of the Redeemer is seen in three parts: Christ has died (Aquila, the pierced Eagle), Christ is risen (Lyra the Harp), Christ will come again (Cygnus the returning Swan). Amazing! (Romans 6:4; 1 Thessalonians 4:13-16)
- He will be exalted above everything as seen in Vega (Philippians 2:9, Ephesians 1:21)
- He will give His people great grace and overcoming power as seen in the star Vega (Acts 4:33; 1 John 5:4)

- The One who is coming back is the same One who died on the cross as seen in Cygnus the Swan and the great Northern Cross
- The One Returning will judge the world in righteous judgement as seen in Deneb (Isaiah 32:1, Psalm 9:8, Psalm 96:13, Psalm 82:8)
- The Judge is returning quickly (Revelation 22:12, Revelation 3:11)
- Deneb in the tail means "the Judge"
- SADR (Hebrew), in the body means "returning"
- Al Bireo in the beak means "quickly"
- He was wounded for our transgressions as sin in Altair (Isaiah 53:5)
- And by His stripes we are healed, as seen in Tarazed (Isaiah 53:5)
- They pierced my hands and my feet, as seen in Alcair (Psalm 22:16)

This is what the heavens declare through the Summer Triangle.

CHAPTER

FIVE

This Is What It All Means

Healthy conclusions and things to ponder

What conclusions can we come to after viewing the story in the heavens? I think God is trusting us with such things as the right conclusions.

> *When I look at your heavens, the work of your*
> *fingers, the moon and the stars, which you have*
> *set in place, what is man that you are mindful of*
> *him, and the son of man that you care for him?*

PSALM 8:3-4 ESV

Mind Blown

This very big plan is the intention of a very, very big God who puts you and me at a very high priority. The pictures in the heavens are meant to be viewed from our perspective. The things these signs represent, the names of the stars and the numbers associated with the science of astronomy all share the same Kingdom themes! The message is clear, the plan is laid out and the Messiah is defined.

The Gift of Realness

I only want to believe what is true. I don't want to waste my time or my life dedicated to something that isn't a reality, and I stand in 100 percent confidence believing God loves me, knows me, and has redeemed me.

Scripture tells us to think on things that are true (Philippians 4:8), and Heaven's progressive revelation of redemption is true, real, and on target with the Kingdom story as laid out in the Bible.

Is it true that Jesus defeated death as the stars prophesied in Aquila and Scorpio? Is it true that He rose again as Sagittarius,

Lyra, and Aries declare? Is it true that He will come back again as Leo and Cygnus proclaim?

I don't mind defending my faith. God commands us to do so in 1 Peter 3:15, telling us to always be ready to let people know why we have so much hope. But how do you argue with the heavens? You can't. What you can argue is that you do not see it, and that is a valid argument. It is a self-incriminating argument of an agenda that is different from wanting to see. Seeing the evidence of God is a choice that every person makes.

Blessed are the pure in heart, for they will see God.

MATTHEW 5:8 NIV

In their song "Already Gone," the Eagles once sang,

Just remember this, my girl,
when you look up in the sky,
You can see the stars
and still not see the light (that's right).

Eyes Wide Open

Since seeing the evidence of God is a choice made in the heart of every living person, it is a pointless exercise to argue the existence of God. God understands that fact and He does not waste His breath arguing His existence.

He has programmed your heart to long for Him. He has programmed your mind to search for Him. He has programmed your body to sense His presence. He has programmed all creation around you to testify of Him, and Romans 1:20 says there is no excuse for not seeing Him. To deny God's existence, I think we have to intentionally shut it all off.

Our "foolish" hearts become darkened when we think we are too smart to believe in God (Romans 1:21). That's why out of 31,170 verses in the written testimony He has given us called the Bible, there is only one verse dedicated as explanation to the agnostic.

The fool has said in his heart, "There is no God."

PSALM 53:1

The other 31,169 verses are given as explanation to those who want to know who God is. Are you one of them? Are you searching Him out?

So when you ask me why I believe in God, I tell you, "Because I want to." The same as those who don't believe, choose not to believe. I have chosen to see the evidence and know MY REDEEMER LIVES!

I can look around and, with barely enough sense to add single-digit numbers, see the design in the perfect order around us—order in our bodies, the ecosystem, time and the seasons and, yes, our solar system. I don't see the random chaos and decay that just happens when you leave things alone, but I see the super intelligent design in the systematic pattern of perfect order.

If there is a Design, there is a Designer!
If there is a Thought, there is a Thinker!
If there is a Plan, there is a Planner!

The plan is revealed through the heavens! This not only tells me there is a God, but this God is a God of purpose, a God of destiny, and He wants to give His power for the benefit of others. Jesus is the fulfillment of the prophecy of the stars.

For we have seen His star in the
East and have come to worship Him.

MATTHEW 2:2

In the midst of all the gods imagined by man, there is only ONE GOD who fits this description. This one God has been revealing a plan throughout the centuries. When Buddha came, there were no prophecies fulfilled that had been spoken for centuries because Buddha was not a part of God's plan. Muhammad fulfilled no prophecies of old because there had never been a revelation from God that He would come to fulfill His plan.

During their lifetimes, they didn't prophesy about their own lives and deaths, and they never fulfilled any prophecy made about them, or by them, because quite simply, they don't know the future. The reason they didn't know the future is because they were not a part of an eternal plan. They did what they did out of personal gain. But Jesus Christ, when He came, He fulfilled 4,000 years worth of prophecy from inspired men and untold millions of years (eternity) as prophesied through the stars and signs in the heavens.

In keeping with His whole prophecy agenda, He Himself prophesied exactly how He would live and how He would die. He gained absolutely nothing, but gave away everything to fulfill His part of an eternal plan.

If there is a Design, there is a Designer!
If there is a Thought, there is a Thinker!
If there is a Plan, there is a Planner!

Jesus told the world that He didn't come to reveal Himself. He came to reveal the Father who sent Him. He came saying, "You have seen the design, now let Me introduce you to the Designer. Let me show you the One whose hand covers the universe and who has named all the stars."

Fifty-Pound Heads

When you are asked to believe that Jesus is Christ, you are not asked to check your brain at the door. You are asked to check your pride. You are asked to check your dignity. You are asked to check your own prejudices and preconceived ideas at the door, and that's what the world is not able to do. God is looking for a people who will choose deity over dignity!

The plan as revealed through the heavens is that the Messiah would come and redeem His people. He would go to war with death, actually die, actually raise from the dead, pour out His Spirit, cause His Church to become one with Him, multiply and bless them, and then He would come back to rule and reign.

If Jesus is the Messiah, the anointed One God made to be a man who is here to complete a perfect task, then the time and place of His appearing must show some evidence of intelligent planning, just like the story in the heavens does. People do not have any control over when they are born, to whom they are born, or to the local, national, or worldwide environment that they are born in. Jesus is the exception.

Jesus Fulfilled at Least 72 Specific Bible Prophesies

Jesus fulfilled biblical prophecies saying who He would be, how He would live, and where He would come from. Prophecies saying that He would have a healing ministry, that He would be crucified with thieves, and even have His clothes gambled over.

A lot of these prophecies seemed to contradict one another. One prophecy said He would be born in Bethlehem, another said He would be called a Nazarene, and another said He would come up out of Egypt. The scribes thought these were all mistakes, and critics thought they were just stupid contradictions. However, Jesus showed up and fulfilled all of them by being born in Bethlehem, fleeing Herod to Egypt, and spending his adult years in Nazareth. Though this was impossible, Jesus Christ fulfilled it.

Another seeming contradiction is that He would be hated, despised, and rejected, but also that He would be buried and honored with the rich. That didn't make sense, but Jesus fulfilled it. Another prophecy said He would be counted among thieves and murderers, yet another said He would be hailed as a King. To the Jews of His time and to many throughput the ages, that doesn't make sense. However, Jesus fulfilled it perfectly.

These things seem impossible, but as Gabriel told Mary when he announced the birth of Christ:

For with God nothing will be impossible.

LUKE 1:37

Jesus Came to Prove That with God, All Things Are Possible

In Psalm 22, there are at least 12 exact prophecies concerning His death, and these things were written 1,000 years before Christ was hanging on the cross. These prophecies include:

- His hands and feet would be pierced.
- He would cry out for thirst.

- What He would say on the cross.

- What the people around would say as He was on the cross, specifically, "He's a big-time truster of God. Let's see if God will deliver Him."

A normal person does not have any control over the events of his death. A normal person is not fulfilling prophecy when he cries out for help. A normal person does not have any control over what the people around him are saying at the time of his death. But this was no normal death. This was an eternal sacrifice prophesied through creation from the very beginning of time. This was no normal man; this was God made Flesh!

This proves once and for all that, yes, there is a God who sits on a very real throne, and He alone knows and controls the future. This same God put His Word and His plan on public display through the pictures we see in the midnight sky and in the names of the stars that display His intentions.

Calling the Shot

In the early part of the last century, there was an incredible baseball player known throughout the United States as Babe Ruth. He wasn't just famous for playing great baseball. He's famous because he said he could do something that was extremely difficult to do, and he said when he would do it.

People were amazed at the concept of a man so confident, that he predicted he would hit the fastball out of the ballpark, and point to where it would land in the bleachers. He "called the shot."

Jesus Christ predicted that He would do the impossible. He predicted that He would raise Himself from the dead. He called the shot when He said that He would do it in three days.

So What's the Big Deal?

Let's look at the facts. The fact that He was born as prophesied, proves He is God. The fact that He fulfilled 353 very specific prophecies, many of which seemed to contradict each other, proves that He is God. The miracles He did, the words He said, how He died and the events surrounding His death—all prophesied long before they happened—prove He is God. Make no mistake: the fact that He rose from the dead, absolutely proves He was, and is, God.

The fact of the matter is, He is real and He is the Fixer of the problem described through the sign Libra. He is Heaven's promised answer from Virgo. He's a Deliverer, a Savior, a Rescuer, an Emancipator, the Ransom, and the Lamb who takes away the sins of the world!

He is a God of power, a God of purpose. He is a God of destiny as described exactly by the signs in the heavens!

If there is a Design, there is a Designer!
If there is a Thought, there is a Thinker!
If there is a Plan, there is a Planner!

You don't have to guess what God is like because He can be seen in the face of a man named Jesus. The Designer, Thinker, and Planner is one altogether beautiful, and for that I am so grateful.

The signs in the heavens are not to be fables and tales, but the epic account of our great Redeemer's love for us.

*For we have not followed cunningly devised fables, when
we made known unto you the power and coming of our
Lord Jesus Christ, but were eyewitnesses of his majesty.*

2 PETER 1:16 KJV

Looking Up: In Conclusion

So the heavenly story finishes with Leo the Lion, and this part of the story has not yet been played out. But we are so close. Closer than you think! The God of breakthrough will soon "crack the sky" as my good friend Mylon Lefevre once sang about. He will come rushing forward as Taurus the Bull with His Church, as the Pleiades declare in these last days:

There will be signs in the sun, in the moon, and in the stars....

LUKE 21:25

A shaking is coming. Things are changing, but you and I are going to be people who are willing to look up.

Now when these things begin to happen, look up and
lift up your heads, because your redemption draws near.

LUKE 21:28

I can see how it might be possible for a man to look down upon the earth and be an atheist, but I cannot conceive how he could look up into the heavens and say there is no God.

ABRAHAM LINCOLN

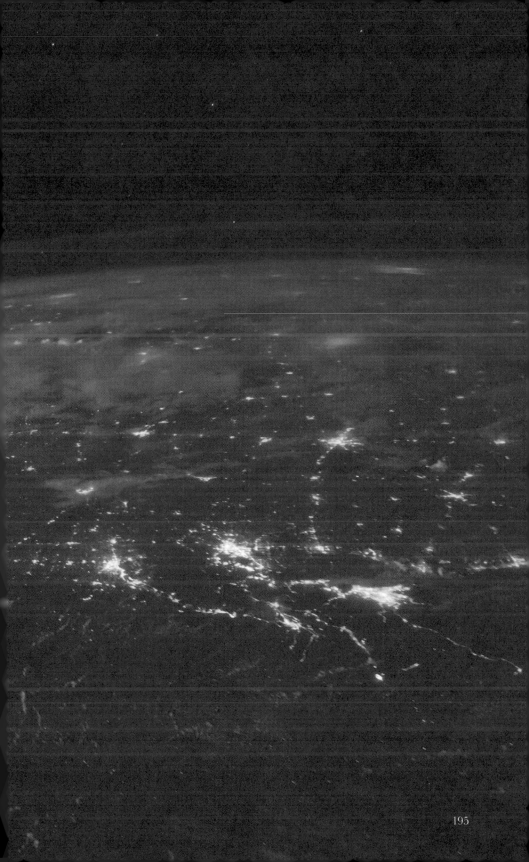

MY CONSTELLATION PRAYER

Even so, come quickly, Lord Jesus (Cygnus). I want to be holy and righteous as You are Holy (Gemini). Make me one as You are One (Capricorn), and never let go of me (Cancer). Pour out Your Spirit upon me and cause me to demonstrate Your power (Aquarius). Let Your Kingdom come and Your will be done in my life (Aries), and rule and reign because Yours is the Kingdom, and the power, and the glory, forever and ever (Leo). In the name of Jesus, my promised Messiah (Virgo), Amen and Amen.

Thank You.

Thanks, Bibliography, and Resources

There has been much made about God's DESIRE for man's fellowship. Yet this has bordered (and frequently crossed the line) on God's NEED for man. God doesn't need anybody. He is completely driven by His passion for us, not for His need.

However, I am not God and this brother has to have lots of help from lots of different sources, and fellowship with lots of different people in order for me to accomplish my mission.

This book is no different. I need to recognize these valuable contributions:

Tommy Owen is mostly responsible for the original illustrative layout of this book. I am so appreciative of him and the design crew of Destiny Image for making this such a stunningly beautiful book.

I have to give a great big Thank You to Kyp Shillam for her research and editing skills. She helps me in so many ways I can hardly count.

OpenDoor Church is still the greatest church in the world to be on staff at. I wrote this book at a very busy time when we were taking on hell with a water pistol on so many different fronts. www.opendoorexperience.com

BIBLE RESEARCH
www.philologos.org
www.biblegateway.com

The Witness of the Stars E. W. Bullinger 1893

http://philologos.org/__eb-tws/

STAR RESEARCH

www.universetoday.com

www.topastronomer.com

www.space.com

www.wikipedia.org

www.davidmalin.com

www.ancient-origins.net

www.almanac.com

www.freestarcharts.com

www.earthsky.org

www.idialstars.com

www.telescope.com

BOOKS ON THIS SUBJECT

The Gospel in the Stars by Joseph A. Seiss

The Heavens Declare: Jesus Christ Prophesied in the Stars
by William D. Banks

God's Voice in the Stars: Zodiac Signs and Bible Truth
by Ken Fleming

The Real Meaning of the Zodiac, Special TBN edition
by D. James Kennedy

*Mystery of the Mazzaroth: Prophecy in the Constellation*s
by Tim Warner

Many Infallible Proofs by Henry M. Morris

*Testimony of the Heavens: God's Redemptive Plan Preserved in the
Stars* by Dana A Sherstad

Taking Back Astronomy: The Heavens Declare Creation
by Jason Lisle

DESTINY IMAGE BOOKS
by Troy Brewer

Redeeming Your Timeline

Redeeming Your Timeline Study Guide

40 Breakthrough Declarations

Other Books by Troy
Brewer at TroyBrewer.com

Best of the Brewer

Miracles with a Message

Good Overcomes Evil & Study Guide

Soul Invasion & Study Guide

Living Life Forward & Study Guide

Numbers that Preach & Study Guide

Next In This Series

LOOKING UP: BOOK TWO

Deeper things revealed and prophetic revelation through the subjects of time, the planets, comets and the three minor constellations of all 12 signs.

How to Contact Troy

TroyBrewer.com

Twitter, Instagram & Facebook: PSTROYBREWER

YouTube: Troy Brewer

Mailing:

PO Box 3775, Burleson, TX 76097

Street:

301 S. Dobson, Burleson, TX 76028

24-Hour Prayer & Resource Line:

877.413.0888

Phone for Booking:

817.319.1300

VIDEO TEACHING ON DEMAND:

ODX.TV

Keep the revelation of LOOKING UP
alive and active in your life
with these prophetic
resources from Pastor Troy:

- Study Guide
- E-Course
- 2-Conference DVD, CD
  or Digital Download
- Pocket Reference Guide
- Prophetic Pictures in the
  Heavens Foldable Map
- Prophetic Art Print
- $5 Downloads for phone

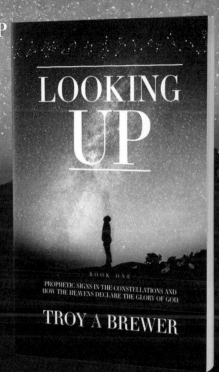

LOOKING UP

BOOK ONE

PROPHETIC SIGNS IN THE CONSTELLATIONS AND
HOW THE HEAVENS DECLARE THE GLORY OF GOD

TROY A BREWER

BE THE FREEDOM FIGHTER YOU WERE MEANT TO BE!

When you partner with Pastor Troy on a monthly basis to rescue girls and boys
from sex slavery worldwide, you'll receive our free gift of ODX.TV. Online and
available 24-7 from anywhere in the world, this teaching platform includes all
Troy's sermons, conferences, podcasts, Wednesday Watch, Daily Devotions, and
Prophetic Numbers videos and so much more! **PARTNER TODAY.**

You'll be transformed and so will they!